AA

Theory Test Made Easy

The step-by-step guide to help you pass the Theory Test

Jane Gregory BA (Hons), PGCE

First published 2002
Reprinted with amendments 2005
Reprinted Mar 2006
Reprinted with amendments 2008

Written by: **Jane Gregory**

Consultants: **Sue Hubbard, ADI, Business Development Manager, AA driving school and Ruth Johnson, Basic Skills Organiser, Reading Adult & Community College**

Copy editor: **Pam Stagg**

Cartoons: **David Baldin**

Additional artwork: **Chris Orr & Associates**

Produced by: **AA Publishing**

© Automobile Association Developments Limited 2008
Video image on page 16 reproduced under licence from the Driving Standards Agency.

Published by AA Publishing (a trading name of Automobile Association Developments Limited, whose registered office is Fanum House, Basing View, Basingstoke, Hampshire RG21 4EA; registered number 1878835). A3784

ISBN-13: 978-0-7495-5743-0

A CIP catalogue record for this book is available from the British Library.

The contents of this book are believed correct at the time of printing. Nevertheless, the publishers cannot be held responsible for any errors or omissions or for changes in the details given in this book or for the consequences of any reliance on the information it provides. This does not affect your statutory rights.

Visit the AA Publishing website at **www.theAA.com/bookshop**

Colour reproduction by: **Keene Group, Andover**
Printed by: **Graficas Estella, Spain**

CONTENTS

How to use this book

This book is designed to help you tackle the questions in the Theory Test part of the driving test. Each chapter includes information to help you understand the questions, as well as sample questions for practice.

To get the best out of this book, you will need a copy of the **Highway Code**. You should also refer to the AA's book, **Driving Test Theory Official Questions and Answers**. This is updated regularly and contains all the real questions you might have to answer in the test. If you are familiar with the real questions, you will be more confident when you have to take your test.

ABOUT THE THEORY TEST

The driving test has two parts:
the Theory Test and the Practical Driving Test.

- The government started the Theory Test because some learner drivers did not understand enough about safe driving.

- The Theory Test is there to find out if you know about the rules of the road and many more important aspects of driving.

- It is easier to understand the Theory Test if you are putting your learning into practice – that is, having lessons in practical driving at the same time as getting ready to take your Theory Test.

Some people are more worried about taking their Theory Test than about taking the Practical Driving Test – and for some it is the other way around.

> ## If you are worried about the Theory Test – read on!

What to expect in the Theory Test

You take the test at a **Theory Test Centre** in your local area. You must contact the centre in advance to fix a time for your test (see page 12).

Apart from signing your name, **you do not have to write anything down**.

The test is in **two parts** and lasts **about an hour**.

Taking the Theory Test

At the Test Centre, you will sit at a computer with the **Theory Test questions** loaded on it.

Video clips for testing Hazard Perception will be on there as well (see pages 13–18).

You need to pass **both** the questions **and** the video test to get a pass in your **Theory Test**.

We'll deal with the 'questions' part first.

Q. What are the questions in the Theory Test like?

- The questions will be like the ones in this book.
- All the questions are **multiple-choice**, and you **touch the answer** you have chosen on the computer screen.

Q. What are multiple-choice questions?

- In multiple-choice questions there are several possible answers listed after the question. You have to choose the one you think is the right answer.

The multiple-choice questions in the Theory Test all have four, five or six answers to choose from.

You will have 57 minutes to do 50 questions. You have to get at least 43 right to pass this part of the Theory Test.

HINTS and TIPS for answering multiple-choice questions

1. **Don't panic!** Maybe you hate exams. Maybe it's a long time since you took an exam. You can still pass the **Theory Test** if you prepare well, with help from your driving instructor.

2. Look at **one question** at a time and try to answer it. **Don't read them all and panic.**

3. **Read the question** first and decide what **you** think the right answer is.

4. If there are any **pictures or diagrams** with the question, study them carefully – they should give you some clues about the right answer.

5. **Read though the answers** and choose the one that seems closest to the answer you had decided on yourself.

If you approach each question like this, you will avoid being confused by answers with similar wording.

IMPORTANT NOTE!

Questions that ask you for two, three or four answers

Look out for questions that ask you to give **two (or more) answers** instead of one.

These will say:

Mark two answers

or: *Mark three answers*

or: *Mark four answers*

The computer will alert you if a question needs more than one answer and you have not answered it in full.

Q. Will the computer be easy to use?

- Only one question appears on the screen at a time, and they are easy to read. You can move backwards and forwards through the questions and 'flag' any that you want to go back to later. You can also change your answer if you need to.

  After you have done this part of the test, you will get a short break of about three to five minutes. Then you will go on to do **the video part of the test.**

Q. What happens in the video test?

- The video part of the Theory Test is known as the **HP element**.

HP stands for **Hazard Perception**. This part (element) of the test lasts about **20 minutes**.

Q. What is Hazard Perception?

- A hazard is anything that might cause you to change speed or direction when driving.

- The aim of the Hazard Perception test is to find out how good you are at noticing hazards coming up on the road ahead.

- The test will also show how much you know about the **risks** of driving. That is,

- risks to you as a driver

- risks to your passengers

- and risks to other road users.

Q. Do I touch the screen when I see a hazard on the video?

- As soon as you see a hazard coming up in the video clip, **you click the mouse control.**

Q. Will I have enough time to see the hazard before the picture changes?

- Don't worry, you will have plenty of time to see the hazard – but the sooner you notice it, the more marks you will score.

(You will find much more on how to do the Hazard Perception test on pages 13–18.)

Q. When will I know whether I have passed the Theory Test?

- You will be told straight away, before you leave the Theory Test Centre. So you won't have to wait for a letter or phone call.

  Remember – keep your **Theory Test Certificate** safe, because you will have to take it with you when you take your Practical Driving Test.

SOME 'DOs' AND 'DON'Ts'

DO prepare for the Theory Test as part of a full course of driving lessons with an instructor from a good driving school. Fully qualified driving instructors are called ADIs (see page 15).

DON'T take the Theory Test before you start practical lessons. You will learn to be a safe driver if you have practical lessons first. Then studying for the Theory Test will make more sense to you.

DO buy an up-to-date book with the real questions in it to help you prepare for the Theory Test. The AA's *Driving Theory Test* book has all the official questions and answers, and is updated every year. It will help you get used to the types of questions that are in the test. It will also help you recognise the key words that come up in the questions.

But – DON'T try to learn all the questions. There are far too many (more than 900). The aim of the Theory Test is to make sure you really understand about driving and safety before you get your full licence to drive.

Always keep a copy of *The Highway Code* handy and read a few pages when you have a spare minute.
If you know your Highway Code it will help you answer the Theory Test questions.

How to prepare yourself for the test

You may be worried about the 'exam' feel of the Theory Test.

Try *not* to worry about this, because:

- The people at the Test Centre will do their best to put you at your ease.
- The computer is easy to use.
- You are doing this for yourself, not for anyone else.
- You will be told the results of your test before you leave the Theory Test Centre.

All you have to do to pass the Theory Test is –
1. Have lessons with a **good driving school** (see page 15)
2. **KNOW YOUR HIGHWAY CODE**.

Feeling OK on the day

Do whatever you know will make you feel most relaxed – go for a walk in the fresh air, or sit down for a while with a newspaper and a cup of tea.

Note: For obvious reasons, this is **not** the time to drink alcohol.

Just before you start the test, take a few deep breaths so that you feel calm, and then begin working steadily through the questions – one at a time.

Q. How do I apply for the Theory Test?

- Find out where your nearest Theory Test Centre is by asking your driving instructor. You can also find out by calling the Driving Standards Agency (DSA) on 0870 010 1372, between 8am and 6pm, Monday to Friday.

- You should get a date and time in about two weeks, though it might be a little longer if you are a driver with special needs. Some centres have appointments on Saturdays and at weekends as well as in the week.

- When you phone you should have ready your **provisional licence** and a **credit or debit card** (the person who books the test must be the card-holder, or the card-holder must be present). If you do not have a card you will be sent an application form and you can pay by postal order or cheque. You can also book on-line at www.dsa.gov.uk

  The cost of the Theory Test is currently £30.00*.

  This cost may change during the lifetime of this book.

Q. I am dyslexic, so I read slowly. Can I have extra time?

- Yes, but the Test Centre will need evidence that you are dyslexic, such as a letter from your school or college.

Q. English is not my first language. Can I do the Theory Test in any language?

- Maybe. The Theory Test is available in some community languages. Contact the DSA to find out.

DSA stands for **Driving Standards Agency**; the organisation set up by the government to promote road safety through better driving. The **DSA** sets all parts of the driving test.

ABOUT THE HAZARD PERCEPTION ELEMENT

Q. Why has HP been added to the Theory Test?

● The HP test has been added to make sure that new drivers know all about hazards and how to look out for them before they are allowed to drive on their own.

● Learner drivers need more training in how to spot hazards, because they are often so busy thinking about using the car's controls that they forget to watch the road and traffic.

● Proper training can really help you to see more of the hazards you will meet when driving, and to see those hazards earlier.

DID YOU KNOW?
In Britain 31,845 people were killed or seriously injured in 2006.

LEARNERS, NEW DRIVERS AND EXPERI-ENCED DRIVERS

Q. Who have the most accidents – new drivers or experienced drivers?

● New drivers have just had lessons, so they should remember how to drive safely. But in fact **new drivers** have most accidents.

Older drivers and younger drivers

In many other skills young people have faster reactions than older people, but this doesn't apply to driving:

Learner drivers and new drivers (those who have passed their Driving Test within the last two years) are up to two seconds slower at spotting hazards than more experienced drivers

– and on average, people aged around 50 have the fastest reactions.

Training can make up for lack of experience: 3–4 hours' training can help learner drivers spot hazards as well as a driver with over 10 years' experience.

How your instructor can help

Your driving instructor has been trained to help you learn hazard perception skills, and can give you plenty of practice in:

- what to look out for when driving

- how to anticipate (be ready for) hazards

- what action to take when you have to deal with hazards of all kinds.

If you have good hazard perception skills you are much less likely to have an accident.

TWO IMPORTANT POINTS!

1. Now that you have to learn about hazard perception before you take the Theory Test, it is even more important to have lessons with a **qualified driving instructor from a good driving school.**

A qualified instructor is called an **ADI**. ADI stands for **Approved Driving Instructor**. It means they have studied and taken a special test themselves. Look for the green ADI certificate on the windscreen of their car.

2. You should **not take your Theory Test too early**. This is because you need the experience of meeting real hazards while you are learning to drive, so that you will be able to pass the HP part of the Theory Test.

However, you must pass the Theory Test before you can take the Practical Driving Test. Agree a plan of action with your driving instructor.

Q. What happens in the HP video test?

- First there is a short talk explaining how the test works; you will also get a chance to practise with the computer and mouse control before you start the test 'for real'. This is to make sure you know what to expect, and that you are happy with what you have to do.

Q. What are the video clips like?

- You will see moving-image clips of a real street scene with traffic such as motor vehicles, pedestrians, cyclists, etc. The scenes are shot from the point of view of a driver in a car. You will see 14 video clips.

- You have to notice **hazards that are developing** on the road ahead– that is, **problems building up that could lead to an accident.**

Q. How many hazards are in each clip?

- Every clip has **at least one hazard** in it – some clips may have more than one hazard.

Pass or Fail

Remember, you have to pass both the questions and
the video part of the Theory Test to get a pass.
At the end of the test they will tell you your scores for
both parts. If you didn't pass, this will help you see where
you need to do better next time.

Q. How many hazards do I have to spot altogether?

- You should find **15 hazards** to 'click' on during the 20 minutes.

Q. Can I go back and change my mind?

- Each test clip will be shown only once, so you must concentrate. You cannot go back to an earlier clip and change your response.

Q. How is the test scored?

- For each hazard you spot you get one or more points.

- You get more or less points depending on how quickly you spot the hazard developing on-screen, and click on it with the mouse.

- You have to score a minimum of 44 out of 75 to pass this element of the theory test.

Note on cheating!

The computer has checks built in to show up anyone trying
to cheat – for example, someone who keeps
clicking the mouse all the time.

IMPORTANT NOTE!

Even if you only 'failed' on one part of the Theory Test, you still have to take both parts again next time.

A practice run

You won't be able to practice with the real video clips used in the test.

This is because the whole idea of the HP element of the Theory Test is to see **how fast you can spot** and **react to hazards**. If you had seen the actual clips before, it would not be a realistic or useful test.

Q. So how can I practice?

- ADIs have **training books and videos** to work through with you during your driving lessons.

- You can also buy a **video and workbook** prepared by the DSA that gives you an idea of what to expect in the HP test.

- The practice video has clips like the real ones you see in the Theory Test.

- You are shown each clip **twice**. The second time you see it, there is a **spoken commentary** to help you learn what to look for – that is, how to spot the hazard in the clip.

- There is also a video clip of an **Introduction** like the one you will get before you do the real test.

1

ALERTNESS

The first section in the Theory Test question books is headed Alertness. Alertness is a short section, so it's a good choice for your first attempt at dealing with the questions.

Q. What does it mean to be alert?

- Alertness means: being wide awake and concentrating on what you are doing – in this case, driving.

- Alertness means: looking out for hazards.

- Alertness means: noticing all road signs and road markings, and acting on the instructions they give.

Tackling the questions

Look at the questions in the **Alertness** section of your Theory Test book.

See if you can pick out the **key word** in each question.

You'll see that the **Alertness** questions are about all these:

- **anticipation**
- **observation**
- **signalling**
- **reversing**
- **using your mirrors**
- **concentration**
- **getting distracted**
- **feeling sleepy**
- **using mobile phones.**

SAMPLE QUESTIONS AND EXPLANATIONS

In the pages that follow, we shall look at some sample questions similar to the ones you will get in the real test.

Each question is followed by an explanation to show you why the right answer *is* the right answer.

At the same time we'll give you extra information about the topic to help you while you are learning to drive.

Note: You'll find more questions that deal with the topics listed above when you get to the section on Hazard Awareness (Chapter 5, pages 51–62), which covers things that might make you feel less alert.

SAMPLE QUESTIONS – ALERTNESS

(1) SAMPLE QUESTION **If you are driving behind a long vehicle you should keep well back. Why is this?**

Mark one answer

☐ A. It leaves you more room if you want to take a corner quickly

☐ B. It allows the driver to see you in their mirrors

☐ C. It shields you from the wind

☐ D. It leaves room for another car to cut in behind the long vehicle

Working out the answer to Question 1

To work out the right answer, **look at the question first and decide what you think the answer is**. Then see if any of those given (**A, B, C** or **D**) fits the answer you have thought of yourself.

Look at the answers in turn:

Answer A   This answer is saying that the reason for holding back is to give you room to turn a corner at speed.

You know from your driving lessons that you should never take a corner too quickly.

Therefore, **Answer A** can't be the right answer.

Answer B   If you are driving too close to a long vehicle, you are hidden from the driver by the vehicle itself. If the driver can see you in their mirrors they will know where you are when they plan to slow down or change direction, and will see if you signal to overtake.

So **Answer B** does not seem to have anything wrong with it – it could be the one to choose.

Answer C

Being shielded from the wind is not a key driving skill. Also, **common sense** tells you that Answer C cannot be right. Obviously if you are well back you are *less* well shielded from the wind. Also, you know that it is not a good idea to drive close behind a long vehicle for *any* reason, as long vehicles need more time and space to stop or change direction than smaller vehicles.

Answer D

It is true that if you are keeping a safe distance behind the long vehicle, this may leave space for another vehicle to cut in and fill the gap. However, that would be bad driving on their part, so this can't be the right answer either.

(1) **_Therefore – B is the right answer._**

That question was about being **alert** and **anticipating** that a long vehicle may need more room.

Now try one about using your skills of **alertness** and **observation**.

The government believes the **attitude** of learner drivers is extremely important for road safety. In the future they might introduce special tests to find out what attitude you have as a driver.

2 **SAMPLE QUESTION** You are driving on a dual carriageway and see a white arrow painted on the centre of the road, curving to the left. What does it mean?

Mark one answer

☐ **A.** Drivers must move on to the hard shoulder
☐ **B.** It tells overtaking drivers there is a bend to the left
☐ **C.** Overtaking drivers must move back to the left
☐ **D.** It is safe to overtake

Working out the answer to Question 2

For a start, this question seems to have something to do with **overtaking**, as that word comes into three of the answers. However, it doesn't come into **Answer A**; could that answer be right?

Answer A The clue to this is in the first part of the sentence – 'You are driving on a dual carriageway'.

A hard shoulder is normally found only on a motorway. And the instruction telling motorists to use the hard shoulder is a large sign high above the carriageway, not a white arrow painted on the road.

So **Answer A** must be wrong.

Answer B Check the signs in your *Highway Code* and you will see that the road sign for a left-hand bend is a black boomerang-shape inside a red triangle.

It's a sign displayed on a pole, not a road marking. So **Answer B** must be wrong too.

(By the way – do you know what the sign is for 'No left turn'? If you're not sure, look that up in your *Highway Code* as well.)

Answer C   A white arrow painted on the road and curving to the left indicates that it's not safe to overtake after that point.

It's a warning to any drivers still overtaking that they should return to the normal road position as soon as they can do so safely.

Answer D   The white arrow is pointing left, to guide you back to the normal road position because it's not safe to overtake. So **Answer D** is wrong.

(2)   *Therefore C is the right answer.*

The remaining sample questions in this chapter are about **concentrating** and not **being distracted** while you are driving.

DID YOU KNOW?
The main causes of distraction are:
– loud music **in the car**
– **passengers (usually** children**)**
– **events happening** outside **(such as accidents)**
– **using a** mobile phone **while driving**

Other sections cover feeling sleepy while driving, and losing concentration due to drink or drugs.

(3)   SAMPLE QUESTION   You have some lucky dice hanging from your interior mirror. They may

Mark two answers

☐ A. Restrict your view
☐ B. Help you drive better
☐ C. Distract you while you are driving
☐ D. Help you to concentrate on your driving

Working out the answers to Question 3

Answer A   The interior mirror is the one inside the car – often called the rear-view mirror.

It stands to reason you need to see as much as possible of the road and traffic around you through your windscreen and in your mirrors so that you can spot hazards. So anything that gets in the way and blocks (restricts) your view is a bad idea.

So **Answer A** could be the right answer.

Answer B   Perhaps if they are 'lucky' dice you think they will help you drive better? But common sense tells that you that **Answer B** is wrong.

Answer C   Anything that moves in front of your eyes could distract you from concentrating on the road. So **Answer C** could be right, too.

Answer D   It's hard to see how something moving about in front of you can help you concentrate; it's much more likely to put you off! So **Answer D** is wrong.

(3) *In this case both A and C are right answers.*

The last question in this section is about using your **mobile phone** while driving.

Note: You might wonder why there are so many questions about one subject, all worded slightly differently. See page 49 for an explanation.

4 SAMPLE QUESTION

If your mobile phone rings while you are on a journey you should

Mark one answer

☐ **A.** Stop the car immediately
☐ **B.** Answer it immediately
☐ **C.** Find a safe place, pull up, and then answer it
☐ **D.** Find a kerb and pull up next to it

Working out the answer to Question 4

Answer A   You would never stop the car immediately just to take a phone call. You have to find a safe place to stop first. Imagine if you were on the outside lane of a motorway – you certainly could not 'stop immediately'. So **Answer A** must be wrong.

Answer B   You should never make calls on your mobile phone while on the move. You should not answer them on the move either. So **Answer B** is wrong.

The best thing is to wait till you can **find a safe place to stop and then deal with the call.**

Better still: make use of **voice-mail** so that the caller can leave a message on your phone and you can call back at a time when you are not driving.

Answer C   Look at the explanation above; **Answer C** sounds like this, so is likely to be right.

Answer D   The important thing to do is to find a *safe* place to pull up. A kerb is not always more safe than, say, a lay-by, or a quiet side road. So **Answer D** is wrong.

4   *So C is the right answer.*

2

ATTITUDE

Q. What is meant by Attitude?

Attitude means:

- your frame of mind when you get into the car

- how you react when you meet hazards on the road

- whether you lose patience or stay calm

- how you behave towards other drivers.

- Attitude is a very important part of being a good driver.

- Your attitude when you are driving plays a big part in ensuring your safety and that of other road users.

Think about these two sentences:

1. I aim to be a careful and safe driver.

2. I aim to be a fast and skilful driver.

Does the first one sound boring to you?

Does the second one sound much more fun?

- Young drivers who have just passed their test often want to drive at high speed, with lots of engine revving, fast acceleration and sharp braking.

  This is probably because they want to show off to their friends.

- Even if you're not a young driver, you might get impatient when you have to wait in a line of traffic, or when you have to drive quite slowly on an empty road because there is a speed limit of 30mph.

What is your attitude to the rules of the road?

Some people think:

- that speed limits are only meant for people who can't react to hazards quickly

- that 'no overtaking' rules are only meant for people who don't have powerful cars.

  Attitudes like these explain why accidents that could be avoided, still happen.

If you don't want to end up as 'just another statistic', **being a safe and careful driver is the only way to go**.

> ## Are you a 'driver with attitude'?

A CAR IS NOT AN OFFENSIVE WEAPON

People often don't realise what a powerful weapon they are in control of when they get behind the wheel of a car.

Think about whether you would ever use your car to fight a battle with another driver.

You only have to think about this to understand how important attitude is in driving.

DEFENSIVE DRIVING IS GOOD DRIVING

Q. What does 'defensive driving' mean?

Defensive driving means:

- anticipating hazards
- showing consideration to other road users
- not taking risks.

DID YOU KNOW?
People aged 19 and under, driving in their first six months have the highest annual accident rates.

Look up the Theory Test questions that come under the heading of **Attitude.** You'll see that they cover many of the points in the **DOs** and **DON'Ts** on the next page, such as:

- tailgating
- consideration for other road users, including pedestrians, buses, slow-moving vehicles and horse riders
- driving at the right speed for the conditions
- when to flash headlights
- the right way to overtake.

Here is a list of DOs and DON'Ts for good drivers.

Good drivers *Do* –

✓ drive at the right speed for the road and traffic conditions

✓ observe speed limits

✓ overtake only when it is safe to do so

✓ park in correct and safe places

✓ wait patiently if the driver in front is not sure of the way, or is a learner

✓ look out for vulnerable road users such as cyclists

✓ concentrate on their driving at all times

✓ plan their journeys so that they have plenty of time to get to their destination.

Good drivers *Don't* –

✗ allow themselves to get involved in 'road rage'

✗ break speed limits

✗ drive too fast in wet or icy weather

✗ accelerate or brake too harshly

✗ overtake and 'cut in', forcing others to brake sharply

✗ put pressure on other drivers by coming up too close behind them (this is called 'tailgating'), flashing headlights, etc.

✗ allow their attention to be distracted by passengers, mobile phones or loud music, or what's happening on the road outside.

SAMPLE QUESTIONS – ATTITUDE

5 SAMPLE QUESTION **What does 'tailgating' mean?**

Mark one answer

- A. Driving while using rear fog lights
- B. Reversing into a parking space
- C. Following too closely behind the vehicle in front
- D. Getting out of a hatchback via the rear door

Working out the answer to Question 5

As you have probably realised by now, usually one of the four answers makes no sense at all. In this case, it's **Answer D.** So you can cross that one off the list straight away.

If you know your *Highway Code*, you can also cross off Answers **A** and **B,** because you know that **tailgating means following too closely behind the vehicle in front**.

5 *So C is the correct answer.*

Q. Why is tailgating dangerous?

- A large number of accidents are cause by **rear-end shunts** – where the vehicle behind crashes into the one in front.

  As well as the risks to life and health, this kind of accident can be very costly, because *the driver behind is nearly always in the wrong and has to pay.*

- You should always leave enough space between your vehicle and the one in front, so that you can stop safely if the driver in front suddenly slows down or stops (see Safety Margins, pages 39–50).

6 SAMPLE QUESTION

You are driving at the right speed for the road you are on, but a driver behind is trying to overtake you. What should you do?

Mark one answer

☐ A. Move into the middle of the road to stop them overtaking

☐ B. Move nearer to the car in front so they have no room to overtake

☐ C. Signal left and wave them on so they can overtake

☐ D. Carry on driving at the speed limit but increase the gap slightly between your vehicle and the one in front.

Working out the answer to Question 6

If you are driving at the right speed and in the right position on the road, there is **no need to change what you are doing**. But pull back a bit from the vehicle in front so if the driver behind insists on overtaking, there is less risk of an accident.

DID YOU KNOW? – if you break the law and collect six or more penalty points on your licence in the two years after you pass your test, you'll lose your licence and have to start again as a learner.

Do not try to stop the car behind from overtaking. Do not move into the middle of the road or move up close to the car in front. These actions could be very dangerous.

You should not give **confusing signals** such as indicating left or waving the other driver on.

6 *So for this question, the right answer must be D.*

3

SAFETY AND YOUR VEHICLE

Go to your book of Theory Test questions and look through the section headed Safety and Your Vehicle.

You will notice that the questions in this section are a bit of a mixture.

They cover many topics about safety, including:

- understanding the controls of your vehicle
- what the car's warning lights tell you
- tyres – correct inflation, pressures and tread depths
- when to switch on hazard warning lights
- passenger safety
- the environment
- security and crime prevention.

Now try going through the section again and see if you can put the questions into groups.

Which ones belong under which of the headings above?

How many questions can you find that are about helping the environment?

SAMPLE QUESTIONS – SAFETY AND YOUR VEHICLE

Let's look at some sample questions from these groups.

Note: Remember that questions on the same topic may appear in more than one section; so, if we don't cover the topic here, it will probably be covered later on in this book.

---

7 **SAMPLE QUESTION** **For which of the following reasons may you switch on hazard warning lights?**

Mark one answer

- [ ] **A.** You need to double-park for a short time
- [ ] **B.** You need to park on double yellow lines
- [ ] **C.** You are being towed
- [ ] **D.** You have broken down

Working out the answer to Question 7

Double-parking means parking your vehicle in the road beside another parked car.

You know from your *Highway Code* that you are not allowed to **double-park** – even for a short time. So the answer cannot be **A**.

In some circumstances you may **stop** on **double yellow lines** (for example, to load or unload goods), but you must not **park** on double yellow lines.

So **B** is also wrong.

Look up all the sections that deal with parking rules in *The Highway Code*. Find out the rules for **red routes, white lines** and **zigzag lines** as well as yellow lines.

What about Answer C?

The rule is, you should never switch on your hazard warning lights while your vehicle is moving. There is only one exception to this rule, and it applies when you are approaching slow or stopped traffic on a motorway. So **C** is wrong.

- Hazard warning lights are just that; they warn other road users of a hazard ahead. So you would need **to switch on your hazard warning lights if you have broken down and your vehicle is causing an obstruction.**

(7)   *Therefore – D is the right answer.*

(8)   **SAMPLE QUESTION**   **What is the legal minimum tread depth for car tyres over three-quarters of the breadth?**

Mark one answer

- ☐ A. 1mm
- ☐ B. 1.6mm
- ☐ C. 2.5mm
- ☐ D. 4mm

Working out the answer to Question 8

This is one of the more **straightforward** questions in the Theory Test, because **you either know the answer, or you don't!**

If you have learned your *Highway Code* you'll know that **Answer B is the right answer** – tyres must have a depth of tread of 1.6 millimetres for at least three-quarters of the width of the tyre ('breadth' is another word for 'width'). This is a **legal** requirement; that means, it's the law.

Note: If you're not sure what 1.6mm looks like, make time to check!

9 **SAMPLE QUESTION**

You have two young teenagers as passengers in your car. Who is responsible for their safety? Is it

Mark one answer

- ☐ **A.** You, the driver
- ☐ **B.** The parents of the teenagers
- ☐ **C.** The teenagers, because they are old enough to look after themselves
- ☐ **D.** Any other adult travelling with you

Working out the answer to Question 9

You can see that **Answer D** does not make sense, because there may not be another adult with you.

As for **Answer B**, even if the parents of the teenagers have asked you to give them a lift, you are still responsible for their safety.

You might think that older children can look after themselves – but the law doesn't see it that way! **Answer C** is wrong too.

9 **The right answer is A:**

– as the driver, you are always responsible by law for the safety of *everyone* travelling in your car.

If any of your passengers are young people under 14, you are responsible for making sure they are wearing seat belts.
You are responsible for them by law even if you are a learner driver yourself.

10 SAMPLE QUESTION **On what part of your vehicle would you expect to find a catalytic converter?**

Mark one answer

☐ **A.** The fuel tank
☐ **B.** The air filter
☐ **C.** The exhaust system
☐ **D.** The cooling system

Working out the answer to Question 10

To answer this, you need to know that cars are fitted with **catalytic converters** to reduce **exhaust emissions**.

Exhaust emissions are the poisonous gases that come out of the vehicle's exhaust and can **harm both people and the environment.** The catalytic converter (or 'cat') will work to make those exhaust fumes cleaner.

- Designers of new cars are working all the time on cleaner systems that do less harm to the environment.

10 *Answer C is the right answer.*

SPECIAL AWARD
FOR THE MOST CONFUSING QUESTION

There's just space to give a special mention to one of the most confusing questions of all time – it must be, because so many learners have phoned the AA to tell us they failed on this question.

The question goes something like this:

What kind of driving results in high fuel consumption?

The answer of course is **bad** driving – especially harsh braking and acceleration. This means that you will use more fuel; and 'high fuel consumption' means using more fuel than you should.

But many people read the word **'high'** as meaning **'good'** – as in 'a high level of driving skill' – and so they end up picking the wrong answer.

AND MORE CONFUSION...

The second most confusing question is the one about **braking distances** and **stopping distances**.

For help with this, see the next chapter, which is about Safety Margins. Always remember that **the stopping distance = the thinking distance + the braking distance**.

Note: If you find some **words** in the questions confusing, look them up in the **Key Words** section at the back of this book.

SAFETY MARGINS

We have mentioned Safety Margins before, when we looked at hazard perception skills 'on the road'.

SAFETY MARGINS AND LEARNER DRIVERS

Experienced drivers are usually better than new or learner drivers at leaving good safety margins. Learner drivers find it harder to keep their vehicle at a safe distance from the one in front.

In this chapter we will look in more detail at what *The Highway Code* has to say about:

- safe stopping distances and
- safe separation distances (these are the same as safety margins).

Safety Margins

Safety margins are an important part of anticipating road and traffic hazards.

Q. What is a safety margin?

- A safety margin is the space you need to leave between your vehicle and the one in front so that you will not crash into it if it slows down or stops suddenly.

Some 34 out of 1000 young new drivers are in serious accidents. For older drivers, the figure is only 7 out of 1000.

- In your *Highway Code* these are called 'Separation Distances' or 'Stopping Distances'. Look them up in the index at the back of *The Highway Code* and find the pages that refer to them. Also look at the table on page 43 of this book.

IMPORTANT NOTE!

When you are learning to drive, you can feel pressured to speed up by drivers behind you.

Don't let other drivers make you cut down on your safety margins. Stay a safe distance behind the vehicle in front. Then you will have enough time to anticipate, and react to, hazards.

The two-second rule

In traffic that's moving at normal speed, allow at least a two-second gap between you and the vehicle in front.

Safe stopping distances

People who are taking their Theory Test often get confused about this.

- Look through the questions in the Safety Margins section of your book of Theory Test questions

- Notice that some of them ask you about your **overall stopping distance**.

Q. What is meant by overall stopping distance?

- **Overall stopping distance** or **stopping distance** is not the same as **braking distance**.

  Stopping distance is made up of

  thinking distance + braking distance

- in other words, the time it takes to notice that there's a hazard ahead plus the time it takes to brake to deal with it.

Here's an example:

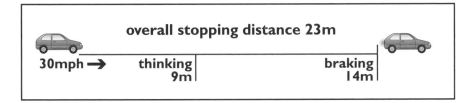

overall stopping distance 23m

30mph → thinking 9m

braking 14m

Thinking distance is sometimes called reaction time
or reaction distance.
If you are driving at 30mph, your thinking distance will be
30 feet. That means your vehicle will travel 30 feet
before you start braking.

Q. What is the link between stopping distance and safety margins?

- You should always **leave enough space** between your vehicle and the one in front. If the other driver has to slow down suddenly or stop without warning, you need to be able to stop safely.

  This **space** is your **safety margin**.

Safety margins for other vehicles

- **Long vehicles and motorcycles need more room to stop** – in other words, you must leave a **bigger safety margin** when following a long vehicle or a motorbike.

- When driving behind a long vehicle, **pull back** to increase your separation distance and your safety margin so that you get a better view of the road ahead – there could be hazards developing.

- Strong winds can blow lorries and motorbikes off course. So leave a **bigger safety margin**.

DID YOU KNOW?
Motorbike riders are vulnerable road users. **In an accident, a biker can be in** more danger **than a car driver. A biker could be thrown on to the road and then be run over by the car behind.**

The basic road safety rule here is:
don't get closer than the overall stopping distance.

Look at the diagram on the next page and try to learn the stopping distances at various speeds.

STOPPING DISTANCES

20 mph

6 metres + 6 metres

= 12 metres (40 feet) or 3 car lengths

30 mph

9 metres + 14 metres

= 23 metres (75 feet) or 6 car lengths

40 mph

12 metres + 24 metres

= 36 metres (118 feet) or 9 car lengths

50 mph

15 metres + 38 metres

= 53 metres (175 feet) or 13 car lengths

60 mph

18 metres + 55 metres

= 73 metres (240 feet) or 18 car lengths

70 mph

21 metres + 75 metres

= 96 metres (315 feet) or 24 car lengths

Thinking Distance

Braking Distance

The average
car length = 4 metres

Note: It's better to learn this table than to have
to learn by your mistakes.
Don't let your experience of near-misses
teach you about safety margins the hard way!

Different conditions and safety margins

One or more questions in your Theory Test might be about driving in 'different conditions'.

These questions aim to make sure you know what **adjustments** (changes) you should make to your driving when either:

road conditions **are different from normal**

– for example, when parts of the road are closed off for roadworks,

or weather conditions **affect your driving.**

Roadworks

You should always take extra care when you see a sign warning you that there are roadworks ahead.

Remember, roadworks are a *hazard* and you have to *anticipate* them.

If you see the driver ahead slowing down, take this as a sign that you should do the same – even if you can't see a hazard ahead. You still need to keep a safe distance from him.

Harassing the driver in front by 'tailgating' is both wrong and dangerous. So is *overtaking* to fill the gap.

Roadworks on motorways

It's especially important that you know what to do when you see a sign for roadworks ahead on a motorway.

- There may be a **lower speed limit** than normal – keep to it.

- Use your **mirrors** and **indicators**, and get into the **correct lane** in plenty of time.

- **Don't overtake** the queue and then force your way in at the last minute (this is an example of showing an inconsiderate **attitude** to other road users).

- Always keep a **safe distance** from the vehicle in front.

Weather conditions

In bad weather (often called 'adverse' weather – weather that's against you!) you need to increase your safety margins.

Look again at the two-second rule on page 40. When it's raining you need to leave at least twice as much room between you and the vehicle in front. When there's ice on the road, leave an even bigger gap.

> *When it's icy you should multiply your two-second gap by ten.*

It's amazing how often drivers go too fast in bad weather. In adverse weather motorways have lower speed limits, but some drivers don't take any notice of them.

You should always obey the signs, and not let yourself be pressured by other people into **driving too fast for the conditions**.

How adverse weather conditions are covered in *The Highway Code* and the Theory Test

You will find three pages on driving in adverse weather conditions in your *Highway Code*. Look these up and read through them, perhaps learning two or three rules at a time.

Now look up the section headed Vehicle Handling in your book of Theory Test questions. You'll see that there are many questions about driving in bad weather in this section, too.

There are questions on two other topics in this section:

- questions on **how to control your vehicle**, especially on downhill slopes
- and questions about **anti-lock brakes**.

Controlling your vehicle

Ask your driving instructor about what you should do when you reach a steep downhill slope. What **gear** should you use? What does **engine braking** mean?

Anti-lock brakes (ABS)

The car you are learning in might not have anti-lock brakes. You still need to know what they can do and how they work.

Can anti-lock brakes always prevent skidding?

**When driving in difficult conditions –
I N C R E A S E   T H E   G A P !**

SAMPLE QUESTIONS – SAFETY MARGINS

11 **SAMPLE QUESTION** **What is your stopping distance at 70mph?**

Mark one answer

- ☐ A 53 metres (175 feet)
- ☐ B 60 metres (197 feet)
- ☐ C 73 metres (240 feet)
- ☐ D 96 metres (315 feet)

Working out the answer to Question 11

Note that you are being asked for your stopping distance **at a fast speed**. 70mph is the top speed for driving on motorways and dual carriageways unless signs show otherwise.

Remember that:
the stopping distance = the thinking distance + the braking distance.

So that gives you a clue that it will be **a long stopping distance**.

If you have learned the table on page 43, you will get **the right answer – Answer D.**

If you find it hard to imagine what the stopping distance at 70mph looks like, here are some tips:
- **The stopping distance at** 70mph **is 96m or** 315ft.
  - **96 metres is about the same length as**
    - **24 cars parked bumper to bumper.**
- **24 car lengths is about the size of a** football pitch.

On a motorway, you can see this distance by looking at the blue marker posts beside the road. They are 100 metres apart – that's almost the same as the 96 metres stopping distance at 70mph!

12 SAMPLE QUESTION **If the weather is very hot, the road surface might get soft. Which of the following would be most affected?**

Mark two answers

- ☐ A The suspension
- ☐ B The steering
- ☐ C The braking
- ☐ D The exhaust

Working out the answers to Question 12

Firstly, if you were reading with care you will have spotted that this question asks you to *mark two answers.*

If you look at the four answers, you'll see that **A** and **D** relate to **mechanical parts of the vehicle**, and **B** and **C** relate **to how you control the vehicle**. This gives you a clue, as any change in the condition of the road surface is most likely to affect your control of the steering or braking.

Your control depends on how well your tyres can grip the road. A dry surface gives more grip than a wet surface, and a firm surface gives more grip than a soft surface.

12 *So the right answers are B and C.*

Questions that look alike

Look up the questions about anti-lock brakes in your book of Theory Test questions. Lots of questions look the same. Some are easy and some are hard.

The questions test two things:

- your knowledge of the rules of the road, and
- your understanding of words to do with driving.

The aim of this book is to help you deal with any words that cause problems for you, so that you can feel confident when you take your Theory Test.

Check that you know what difficult words mean by looking at the Key Words section at the back of this book. It explains what terms like **defensive driving** and **high-sided vehicle** mean, as well as words such as **priority** and **tailgating**.

> **13** SAMPLE QUESTION **In normal driving conditions on a fast road in good weather, the distance for safety between you and the vehicle in front should**
>
> **?**
>
> *Mark one answer*
> - ☐ **A** One car length
> - ☐ **B** Two car lengths
> - ☐ **C** 2 metres (6 feet 6 inches)
> - ☐ **D** A two-second time gap

Working out the answer to Question 13

You'll most likely have spotted straight away that this question is about our old friend the **two-second rule** (see page 40). To check that the others are wrong, remember the **table of stopping distances** (see page 43).

> **13** *So you can be pretty sure that the right answer is D.*

The stopping distance at 70mph is equal to 24 car lengths, so **Answers A** and **B** don't come near. As for **Answer C**, you know that 2 metres or 6 feet 6 inches is only slightly more than the height of a tall person, so you can cross off that one too.

When you are driving it is easier to judge distances in **time** rather than in yards or metres. Remember that the **faster** you are going the **more time** (distance) you will need to stop.

HAZARD AWARENESS

Q. What is the difference between Hazard Awareness and Hazard Perception?

- **Hazard Awareness** and **Hazard Perception** mean the same thing.

- Hazard Perception is the name for the new part of the Theory Test that uses video clips. This test is about spotting developing hazards. One of the key skills of good driving, this is called **anticipation.**

- Anticipating hazards means **looking out for them in advance and taking action _now_.**

- Hazard Awareness is about being **alert** whenever you are driving.

That is why some of the questions in this Hazard Awareness section deal with things that might make you less alert – for example:

- feeling tired

- feeling ill

- taking medicines prescribed by your doctor

- drinking alcohol.

Other questions in this section cover:

- noticing road and traffic signs and road markings

- what to do at traffic lights

- when to slow down for hazards ahead.

Taking action to avoid accidents

New drivers have a greater than average chance of being involved in accidents.

Young male drivers have the most accidents.

Q. Why are young male drivers more at risk?

- Maybe it's because when they get their licence they want to show off to other drivers.

- Some people think that driving much too fast will earn them 'respect' from their friends.

- Some people think that they are such good drivers, the rules of the road don't apply to them.

Whatever the reason – *drivers who don't watch out for hazards are at risk of being involved in an accident.*

The problem has a lot to do with people's **attitude** to driving; you'll find more about the part of the Theory Test that deals with attitude on pages 27–32 of this book.

We've already said that young drivers often don't learn to anticipate hazards until they are older and more experienced.

The HP test aims to 'fill the gap' in hazard perception for young drivers and other new drivers by making sure they have some proper training to make up for their lack of experience.

This should make them safer drivers when they start out on the road alone.

- Drivers **under 25 make up only 9%** of all full licence holders.
- Young drivers don't drive as many miles as older drivers. But they are involved in 29% of accidents where someone is hurt or seriously injured.

Looking for clues to developing hazards

As you get more driving experience you will start to learn about the times and places where you are most likely to meet hazards.

Think about some of these examples:

Rush hour

You know that people take more risks when driving in the rush hour. Maybe they have to drop their children off at school before going to work. Maybe they are late for a business meeting. So you have to be prepared for bad driving, such as other drivers pulling out in front of you.

Dustbin day

Drivers in a hurry may get frustrated if they are held up in traffic because of a hazard such as a dustcart. They may accelerate and pull out to overtake even though they cannot see clearly ahead. You should not blindly follow the lead of another driver. Check for yourself that there are no hazards ahead.

School children

Young children are not very good at knowing how far away a car is from them, and may run into the road unexpectedly. Always be on the lookout for hazards near a school entrance.

Parked cars

Imagine you are driving on a quiet one-way street with cars parked down each side. You wouldn't expect to meet any vehicles coming the other way – but what about children playing? They might run out into the road after a football. It would be difficult to see them because of the parked cars, until they were in the road in front of you.

> **Don't forget: not all hazards can be anticipated.**
> **There are bound to be some you haven't expected.**
> ALWAYS EXPECT THE UNEXPECTED!

Scanning the road

Learner drivers tend to look straight ahead of their car and may not notice all the hazards that might be building up **on both sides.**

You will spot more hazards when driving if you train yourself to **scan the road.**

- Practice looking **up and ahead** as far as possible.

- Use all your mirrors to look out for hazards too.

- Don't forget you have 'blind spots' when driving – work out where they are and find safe ways of checking all round for hazards.

- Ask your driving instructor to help you with all this.

Q. How is learning to scan the road going to help me pass my Theory Test?

- As we have said before, the idea of the HP element is to encourage you to get some real experience of driving before you take the Theory Test.

- If you meet real hazards and learn how to anticipate them, you'll learn how to pass the hazard perception part of the test.

- In the video test you may not be able to look **all around you** as you would when driving a car; but the clips will be as realistic as possible in giving you a wide 'view' of the road ahead.

MORE EXAMPLES OF HAZARDS

So, what kinds of hazards are we talking about? And what should you do about them?

The list below gives some of the hazards you should look out for when driving along a busy street in town.

After each hazard there are some ideas about what you should be looking out for, and what to do next.

- *You see a bus which has stopped in a lay-by ahead.*

> **There may be some pedestrians hidden by the bus who are trying to cross the road, or the bus may signal to pull out. Be ready to slow down and stop.**

Road markings and road signs sometimes highlight likely hazards for you.

- *You see a white triangle painted on the road surface ahead.*

> **This is a hazard warning sign. It tells you that there is a 'Give Way' junction just ahead. Slow down and be ready to stop.**

- *You see a sign for a roundabout ahead.*

> **Anticipate that other drivers may need to change lane, and be ready to leave them enough room.**

- *You come to some road works where traffic is controlled by temporary traffic lights.*

> **Watch out for drivers speeding to get through before the lights change.**

Hazards may be all around you – not just in front.

- *You look in your rear view mirror and see an emergency vehicle with flashing lights.*

    An emergency vehicle wants to pass, so get ready to pull over when it's safe.

Not all hazards are on the road.

- *You see a small child standing with an adult near the edge of the pavement.*

    Check if the child is safely holding the adult's hand. Be ready to stop suddenly if the child steps into the road.

- *You notice dustbins or rubbish bags put out on the pavement.*

    The dustcart could be around the next corner, or bin men could be crossing the road with bags of rubbish. Be ready to slow down.

Remember to listen for hazards, too.

- *You hear a siren.*

    Look all around to find out where the emergency vehicle is. You may have to pull over to let it pass.

You will find out more about different types of hazards, such as what to look for when driving in the country, or in bad weather, in Vehicle Handling, pages 77–82.

Observation

Another word for taking in information through our eyes is observation.

Observation is one of the three key skills needed in hazard perception:

- **observation**
- **anticipation**
- **planning.**

An easy way to remember this is **O A P** for

Observe – Anticipate – Plan.

Talking to yourself again?

It's a good idea to 'talk to yourself' when you're learning to drive – and even after you've passed your test. Talk about all the things you see that could be hazards. Your driving instructor might suggest this as a way of making you concentrate and notice hazards ahead.

Even if you don't talk out loud, you can do a 'running commentary' in your head on everything you see around you as you drive.

For example, you might say to yourself –

'I am following a cyclist and the traffic lights ahead are red. *When the lights change I shall allow him/her plenty of time and room to move off.*'

or

'The dual carriageway ahead is starting to look very busy. There is a sign showing that the right lane is closing in 800 yards. *I must get ready to drop back, to allow other vehicles to move into the left-hand lane ahead of me.*'

Note: Don't forget the mirrors! This way, you will notice more hazards, and you will learn to make more sense of the information that your eyes are taking in.

Observation questions

Go to your book of Theory Test questions and study some of the pictures in the Hazard Awareness section.

They include **photographs** of scenes such as:

- a cyclist at traffic lights, seen from the viewpoint of a driver in a car behind the cyclist

- what you see as a driver when you are approaching a level crossing

- what you see when coming up to a 'blind bend'

- a view of the road ahead with traffic building up where one lane is closing.

DID YOU KNOW? Our eyes can take in 30–40 images per second. We have to make sense of these images, and decide what to do next.

Look out for situations like these when you are out driving with your instructor, and **use the practice to improve your hazard awareness.**

People who have been driving for longer have fewer accidents than new drivers. What's the reason?
- better Hazard Perception skills!

As well as photographs, there are **pictures** of **road and traffic signs**.

Look at these examples:

What do these signs mean?

What actions should you take when you see these signs?

- If you are not sure, look them up in your *Highway Code*.

- Think about *why* the square yellow sign with the two children is in the Vehicle Markings section and not with the rest of the road signs.

Learn your road signs!

Notice the information in your *Highway Code* at the bottom of the first page of road signs. It explains that **you won't find every road sign shown here**.

You can buy a copy of *Know Your Traffic Signs* from a bookshop to see some of the extra signs that are not in *The Highway Code*.

Note: In Wales, some signs have the Welsh spelling as well as the English; and in Scotland, some signs have Gaelic spelling. You'll also see some 'old-style' road signs around, which are slightly different too.

SAMPLE QUESTIONS – HAZARD AWARENESS

14 **SAMPLE QUESTION** While driving, you see a sign that looks like this ahead. What would you expect drivers ahead of you to do?

GET IN LANE

400 yards

Mark one answer

- ☐ A Move into the right lane
- ☐ B Speed up to get ahead
- ☐ C Move into the left lanes
- ☐ D Carry on as normal

Working out the answer to Question 14

Answer A suggests traffic might move into the right lane. This can't be correct, because **it's the right lane that's about to close.** So Answer A is wrong.

Answer B is correct in one way – drivers often speed up and overtake to get in front of others when one lane is about to close. But you know from your own experience that motorists who do this are being selfish and showing **no consideration** for other road users. They will force following drivers to slow down, instead of allowing the traffic to keep flowing. So, **Answer B is wrong**.

If drivers in the right lane were to make **no adjustments at all** to their speed or direction, they would soon be in trouble when the lane closed. So **Answer D** is wrong.

As the right lane is going to close, drivers must use their mirrors and indicators to **move across into the left lanes in good time, when it is safe to do so.**

14 *Answer C is the right answer.*

(15) **SAMPLE QUESTION**

You see a set of two amber lights on a pole flashing alternately. What hazard should you look out for?

Mark one answer

- ☐ A A level crossing with no gate or barrier
- ☐ B A swing bridge
- ☐ C An ambulance station
- ☐ D A school crossing patrol

Working out the answer to Question 15

Look up the rules that deal with Level Crossings in your *Highway Code*. Study the diagram that shows a car waiting at crossing gates.

Level crossings, ambulance stations and swing bridges all have **red lights that flash on and off** to warn you when you must stop.

But this question is about flashing **amber** lights.

(15)

Amber lights warn of a school crossing patrol, so Answer D is right.

- Do you know what a **swing bridge** looks like? If there are none near where you live, ask your driving instructor if there are any nearby that you could go and see.

- A **fire station** is another place where you will see red flashing warning lights.

16 SAMPLE QUESTION **Which THREE of the following are likely effects of drinking and driving?**

Mark three answers

- A Improved concentration
- B Poor judgement
- C Lack of coordination
- D Colour blindness
- E Improved reaction times
- F Increased confidence

Working out the answers to Question 16

Firstly, note that this questions asks you to mark **THREE** answers. (When you take your Theory Test the computer will alert you if you don't do this.)

To answer this question correctly you need to know what all the words mean. **'Effects'** means **results** – so it's asking what will happen to your driving skills if you drink alcohol.

Drinking alcohol **will not** improve your concentration – that is, it won't help you concentrate better. So **Answer A** is wrong.

It **will** make you worse at making decisions ('poor judgment'). So **Answer B is one of the three right answers.**

Lack of coordination means not being able to control your own movements properly. Drinking can cause this, so **Answer C is another right answer.**

Colour-blindness is not caused by drinking alcohol, so **D** is wrong.

Your reaction times will get *worse* not *better*, so **E** is wrong.

You *will* feel more confident. But alcoholic confidence is the wrong kind and leads to taking risks. So **Answer F is the third right answer.**

VULNERABLE ROAD USERS

Q. What does 'vulnerable road users' mean?

- **A vulnerable road user is somebody who is at risk from other road users.**

Vulnerable road users include:

- pedestrians
- children
- elderly people
- people with disabilities
- cyclists
- motorcycle riders
- horse riders
- learner drivers
- new drivers
- animals being herded along the road.

You must drive with extra care when you are near vulnerable road users.

THIS SECTION EXPLAINS

- why different types of road users are vulnerable (at risk)

- what you as a driver must do to keep them safe.

Vehicle safety and vulnerable road users

Today's vehicles are getting safer all the time for the driver *inside* the car – but not always for the pedestrian, cyclist etc *outside*.

Many road users who are not driving cars have nothing to protect them if they are in an accident with a motor vehicle.

Cyclists and motorcycle riders

Cyclists and motorcycle riders are more at risk than car drivers because:

- they are more affected by strong winds, or by turbulence (movement of air) caused by other vehicles
- they are more affected by an uneven road surface, and they may have to move out suddenly to avoid a pot-hole
- car drivers often cannot see them.

Always give cyclists plenty of room –

especially when they are **coming up to a roundabout**.

Unlike car drivers, cyclists can stay in the left lane on a roundabout while signalling right as they pass an exit, to indicate that they are carrying on round (see the rules for cyclists in your *Highway Code*).

Turn to the section headed Vulnerable Road Users in your book of Theory Test questions to see some pictures of this.

Other places where cyclists have priority

You must also give way to cyclists:

- at **toucan crossings**
- in **cycle lanes.**

Pedestrians

Pedestrians most at risk include **elderly people** and **children**.

Elderly people and others who cannot move easily may be slower to cross roads – you must give them plenty of time.

Children don't have a sense of danger on the road; they *can't tell how close a car is, or how fast it is going*. They may run out into the road without looking. Or they may step out behind you when you are reversing – you may not see them because they are small.

People who cannot see or hear are especially vulnerable road users. Look out for blind people **with** white sticks. People who are both blind and deaf **carry a white stick with a red band, to tell you they have no warning of cars from engine noise.**

When to give way to pedestrians

At any pedestrian crossing, if a pedestrian has started to cross, wait until they have reached the other side. Do not harass them by revving your engine or edging forward.

- **On a light-controlled pedestrian crossing**

    At a crossing with lights (pelican, toucan or puffin crossings), pedestrians have priority once they have started to cross even if, when on a pelican crossing, the amber lights start flashing.

- **On a zebra crossing**

    Once the pedestrian has stepped on to the crossing you must stop and wait for them to cross.

Note: It is courteous to stop at a zebra crossing if a pedestrian is waiting to cross. When you take your Practical Driving Test, you must stop for any pedestrians who are waiting on the pavement at a zebra crossing – even if they haven't stepped onto the crossing yet. However, you must not wave to them to cross.

- **When they have started to cross a road that you want to turn into**

If you want to turn left into a side road and people are crossing the side road on foot, wait for them to finish crossing

– people on foot have priority over car drivers.

DID YOU KNOW?
If a car hits a pedestrian at 40mph, the pedestrian will probably be killed.
Even at 30mph, 50% of pedestrians hit by cars will be killed.
At 20mph, pedestrians have a better chance of surviving. This is why you will find 20mph limits and other things to slow traffic in some residential streets and near school entrances.

Other types of vulnerable road users

Be prepared to slow down for **animals, learner drivers**, and other more unusual hazards such as people **walking along the road in *organised* groups** (for example, on a demonstration, or a sponsored walk). There are rules in *The Highway Code* that walkers must follow – you'll find these towards the front of your *Highway Code*. But even if they break the rules, make sure you keep to them.

Animals

Drive slowly past horses or other animals. Allow them plenty of space on the road.

Don't frighten them by sounding your horn or revving your engine.

If you see a flock of sheep or a herd of cattle blocking the road, you must:
- stop
- switch off your engine
- and wait until they have left the road.

SAMPLE QUESTIONS – VULNERABLE ROAD USERS

17 **SAMPLE QUESTION** **You are approaching a zebra crossing and see a person in a wheelchair waiting to cross. You should**

Mark one answer

- A Carry on driving
- B Wave them across
- C Signal to them to wait
- D Prepare to stop

Working out the answer to Question 17

When you see a person waiting to cross at a zebra crossing **you should stop for them**. It does not matter whether they are on foot or in a wheelchair, you should still stop. **So Answer A is wrong**.

You should not wave anyone across at a pedestrian crossing; you might put the pedestrian in danger. For example, another car could overtake yours illegally and run into the pedestrian. **So Answer B is wrong**.

You should not make any signal to the pedestrian – do not signal to them to wait, because **they have priority** on the crossing. **So Answer C is wrong**.

17 *Answer D is right – you should prepare to stop.*

18 **SAMPLE QUESTION** **You are about to turn left into a side road. You see that pedestrians have started to cross the side road. You should**

Mark one answer

☐ **A** Keep moving but give them plenty of room
☐ **B** Stop and wave them across
☐ **C** Give way to the pedestrians
☐ **D** Sound your horn and proceed

Working out the answer to Question 18

If you keep moving you risk running into the pedestrians; they may stop suddenly, or change direction. **So Answer A is wrong**.

Answer B is also wrong – you should not wave them across, but leave the pedestrians **to take care of their own safety**.

If you sound your horn (**Answer D**) you are harassing the pedestrians, **so Answer D is wrong**.

Pedestrians crossing a side road **have priority**, so you should **give way** to them.

18 *Therefore – C is the right answer.*

7

OTHER TYPES OF VEHICLE

We have already come across some of the other types of vehicles that share the road with you and your car.

These include **motorbikes** and **bicycles**.

The questions in this part of the Theory Test are mostly about motorbike riders and cyclists. However, you also need to know what to do about other vehicles, such as:

- buses

- caravans

- trams

- tractors and other farm vehicles

- special vehicles for disabled drivers (powered invalid carriages)

- slow vehicles such as road gritters

- motorway repair vehicles.

Important points to remember about these other types of vehicle:

- **many of them can only move very slowly**

- **they cannot easily stop or change direction.**

  The driver's field of vision may be **restricted** – in other words, the driver cannot see clearly in all directions. This means that car drivers have to **change their driving** to allow them plenty of room.

Cyclists

Give cyclists plenty of room

Remember to **keep well back** from cyclists when you are coming up to a junction or a **roundabout** because you cannot be sure what they are going to do.

On the roundabout they may go in *any direction* – left, right, or straight ahead.

They are allowed to *stay in the left lane* and signal right if they are going to continue round.

Leave them enough room to *cross in front of you* if they need to.

Cyclists and strong winds

Remember, two-wheeled vehicles are easily blown off-course by strong crosswinds. So allow plenty of space when you overtake a cyclist, in case they swerve suddenly.

Look out for cyclists!

- It can be **hard to see** cyclists in busy **town traffic**.
- It can also be hard to see them coming when you are waiting to turn out at a **junction**. They can be hidden by other vehicles (see below).

Always be on the lookout for cyclists. Especially, **check your mirror** to make sure you do not trap a cyclist on your left when you are turning left into a side road.

- Check your **blind spots** for cyclists, too.

Controlling your vehicle near cyclists

When you are following a cyclist, you must be able to drive **as slowly as they do**, and keep your vehicle under control. Only overtake when you can allow them plenty of room, and it is safe to do so.

> # Cycle lanes
>
> Cycle lanes are for cyclists. Car drivers should not use them. A cycle lane is marked by a **white line** on the road. A **solid white line** means **you must not drive or park in the cycle lane** during the hours it is in use. A **broken white line** means you should drive or park in it **only if there is no alternative**. You should not park there at any time when there are **waiting restrictions**.

Motorcycles

- Motorcycles are easily blown off course by strong winds.

  If you see a motorcyclist overtaking a **high-sided vehicle** such as a lorry, keep well back. The lorry may shield the motorcyclist from the wind as it is overtaking, but then a sudden gust could blow the motorcyclist off-course.

- It can be **hard to see** a motorcyclist when you are waiting at a **junction**. Always look out for them.

- If you see a motorcyclist **looking over their shoulder**, it could mean that they will **soon give a signal to turn right**. This applies to cyclists too. Keep back to give them plenty of room.

- Motorcyclists and cyclists sometimes have to **swerve to avoid hazards** such as bumps in the road, patches of ice and drain covers. As before – give them plenty of room.

When you overtake a cyclist, a motorcyclist or a horse rider, give them at least as much room as you would a car.

Long vehicles

- Like cyclists, long vehicles coming up to roundabouts may *stay in the left lane even if they intend to turn right.*

This is because they need lots of **room to manoeuvre (turn).**

Keep well back so they have room to turn.

- Take great **care when overtaking** long or high-sided vehicles.

Before you pull out to overtake, make sure you have *a clear view of the road ahead.*

Buses and trams

- Always **give way to buses** when they signal to pull out.

- Always **give way to trams**; they cannot steer to avoid you.

- Don't try to **overtake** a tram.

Trams are **quiet** vehicles – you cannot rely on engine noise to warn you that a tram is coming.

Take extra care when you see this sign, because **trams are sometimes allowed to go when car drivers are not**.

Tractors and slow-moving vehicles

● Always **be patient** if you are following a slow vehicle.

Drivers of slow vehicles will usually try to find a safe place to pull in to let the traffic go past. Keep well back, so that you can see the road ahead. Allow a safe distance in case they slow down or stop.

Slow vehicles are not allowed on motorways because they cannot keep up with the fast-moving traffic. Vehicles not allowed on motorways include:

motorcycles under 50cc

bicycles

tractors and other farm vehicles

powered invalid carriages.

For more on Motorway Rules, see pages 83–90 of this book.

SAMPLE QUESTIONS – OTHER TYPES OF VEHICLE

19 **SAMPLE QUESTION** **You are following a motorcyclist who is travelling slowly. Which of the following signs alerts you to take special care?**

Mark one answer

- [ ] A.
- [ ] B.
- [ ] C.
- [ ] D.

Working out the answer to Question 19

Look up these signs in your *Highway Code*. You will see that that **Sign A** means 'side winds', **Sign B** means 'no left turn', sign **C** means 'one-way traffic' and **Sign D** means 'no stopping (clearway)'.

You know that strong side winds can blow a motorcyclist off course. **Sign A** is the sign for high winds.

19 *So Answer A is the right answer.*

20 SAMPLE QUESTION **You are following a long vehicle coming up to a crossroads. The driver of the long vehicle signals left, but moves to the right towards the middle of the road. What should you do?**

Mark one answer

- [ ] A Accelerate to pass the long vehicle before it starts to turn
- [ ] B Wait until it starts to slow down before you overtake
- [ ] C Stay well back to give the long vehicle plenty of room
- [ ] D Assume the signal is wrong – it is actually going to turn right

Working out the answer to Question 20

Answers A, B and **D** are all **very dangerous** actions. If you try to overtake you will endanger yourself and other road users.

A long vehicle needs plenty of room to go round a corner, so may need to pull out into the centre of the road before making the turn.

20 *Therefore – C is the right answer.*

21 SAMPLE QUESTION **You see a bus ahead signalling to move off. You should**

Mark two answers

- [ ] A Carry on at the same speed but use your horn
- [ ] B Slow down and allow the bus to pull out in front of you
- [ ] C Accelerate past the bus before it moves out
- [ ] D Look out for pedestrians appearing suddenly

Working out the answers to Question 21

You should **always give way to a bus** which is signalling to pull out. So **Answer A** and **Answer C** are both wrong; and **Answer B is one of the two right answers**.

It is common sense that when you follow a bus you should **keep a look-out for pedestrians** crossing in front of or behind the bus.

21 *So Answers B and D are the two right answers.*

22 **SAMPLE QUESTION** **You are driving on a road where there are tram lines. Why should you take extra care?**

Mark two answers

☐ A Trams do not stop for cars
☐ B Trams have no lights
☐ C Trams cannot steer to avoid you
☐ D Trams can approach silently

Working out the answers to Question 22

Answer A is not true, although sometimes trams may have priority over cars. **Answer B** is obviously nonsense: trams need to have lights like any other vehicle on the road.

Trams have to run on tram lines, so they **cannot steer to avoid you**. Because they are electric, they **make hardly any noise**, so you may have no warning that they are there.

22 *So Answers C and D are the two right answers.*

VEHICLE HANDLING

The questions in this section test how much you know about controlling your vehicle.

Your control is affected by:

- the **road surface** – is it rough or smooth? Are there any holes or bumps? Are there any 'traffic-calming measures' such as humps or chicanes?

- the **weather conditions** – you have to drive in different ways when there is fog, snow, ice or heavy rain.

Other questions cover

- **driving on country roads** – on narrow and one-way roads, humpback bridges, steep hills, fords.

There are also questions that need **technical knowledge** – for example, *on engine braking, brake fade*, and *coasting your vehicle.*

This section also has some questions on **overtaking** and **parking**.

Road surface

- The **condition** of the road surface can affect the way your vehicle handles (drives on the road).

Your vehicle handles better on a smooth surface than on a surface that is damaged, bumpy or full of holes. If you have to drive on an uneven surface, **keep your speed down** so that you have full control of your vehicle, even if your steering wheel is jolted.

Take care also where there are **tramlines** on the road.

- The **layout** of the road affects the way your vehicle handles.

You may have to adjust your driving for traffic calming measures such as **traffic humps** (sometimes called 'sleeping policemen') and **chicanes**. These are double bends that have been put into the road layout to slow the traffic down. The sign before the chicane tells you *who has priority*.

Traffic calming measures are often used in residential areas or near school entrances *to make it safer for pedestrians*.

Weather conditions

Bad weather (adverse weather) such as **heavy rain, ice** or **snow** affects the way your vehicle handles. **If you drive too fast** in adverse weather, your tyres may lose their grip on the road when you try to brake. This means the car may skid or 'aquaplane'.

- Aquaplaning means sliding out of control on a wet surface.

Remember the two-second rule?

You should **double** the two-second gap to **four seconds** when driving in rain, and increase the gap by as much as **ten times** when there is **ice** on the road.

Q. What are the rules for driving in snow?

- In snow, the best advice is **do not drive at all** unless you really have to make a journey. If you have to drive in snowy conditions, leave extra time for your journey and keep to the main roads.

- You can fit **snow chains** to your tyres to increase their grip in deep snow.

Q. What about driving in fog?

- In fog your *field of vision* can be down to a few metres.

   Your vehicle is fitted with **fog lights** to help you see and be seen in fog. But you must know *how and when to use them*.

- Look up the three rules about fog lights in your *Highway Code*. You'll see that the key points to remember are:

   – *don't dazzle other road users with your fog lights*

   – *and switch them off as soon as you can see better* (once visibility improves).

Country driving

If you have had most of your driving lessons in a town, you need to know how to drive on **narrow country roads**. Some are only wide enough for one vehicle ('single-track'), and some are on very steep hills.

Your control of the **gears, clutch and brakes** will be important if you have to follow a tractor very slowly **up a hill.** On a **steep downward slope** you have to make sure your vehicle does not 'run away'.

On country roads you might find **humpback bridges** and **fords**. The signs below warn you of these hazards.

● Find out what you must do *first* after you have driven through a ford.

Technical knowledge

We have already mentioned **engine braking.** Understanding how engine braking works is part of good vehicle handling.

Note: If you press the footbrake constantly on a long hill, you may get brake fade. If you're not sure, check what that means in the **Key Words** at the back of this book.

Use the gears to control your vehicle on a downhill slope (or 'gradient'). If you put the vehicle in 'neutral', or drive with the clutch down, and **coast** down the hill your vehicle will increase speed beyond what is safe.

> ● *Coasting is wrong and dangerous* – you should not be tempted to do it to save fuel.

Look back to page 37 for another example of a question where you have to use your technical knowledge. Question 12 on page 48 was about the fact that **hot weather can affect the way your vehicle handles**, because the road surface can become **soft**.

Remember that if there is **sudden heavy rain** after a dry hot spell, the road surface can get very **slippery**.

SAMPLE QUESTIONS – VEHICLE HANDLING

23 **SAMPLE QUESTION** **When travelling in conditions of heavy rain, your separation distance should be**

Mark one answer

☐ A halved
☐ B multiplied by two
☐ C up to ten times greater
☐ D the same as in normal conditions

Working out the answer to Question 23

If you have learned the **two-second rule**, you should have no problem with this question. Your separation distance should be doubled or 'multiplied by two'.

Answer A must be wrong because 'halved' means 'divided by two'.

Answer C would be right if the question was about driving in icy conditions, when you have to multiply your safety margin by ten.

The question asks about driving in 'heavy rain', so **Answer D** is unlikely to be right.

23 *Answer B is the right answer.*

24 **SAMPLE QUESTION** **What do traffic calming measures do?**

Mark two answers

☐ A They tell drivers when to overtake
☐ B They reduce road rage
☐ C They slow down the traffic
☐ D They increase pedestrian safety

Working out the answers to Question 24

Traffic calming measures include speed humps, chicanes and **rumble strips**. They are there to make traffic slow down.

You should not overtake where there are traffic calming measures, so **Answer A** is wrong. **Answer B** is wrong too: road rage means angry drivers, and this question is about **calming** traffic.

(24)   *Answers C and D are the two right answers.*

(25) SAMPLE QUESTION   **What rule applies to the use of fog lights?**

Mark one answer

- ☐ A Use them only in heavy traffic
- ☐ B Never use them on motorways
- ☐ C Only use them with dipped headlights
- ☐ D Remember to turn them off once visibility improves.

Working out the answer to Question 25

Answer A does not make sense – you might be driving on a lonely country road in fog and need to switch on fog lights. So Answer **A** is wrong.

You may need to use fog lights on a motorway in very heavy fog, so **Answer B** is wrong. But you should always switch them off as soon as the fog starts to clear, so that you *do not dazzle other drivers.*

There is no rule in *The Highway Code* about using fog lights with dipped headlights. You have to decide what will best help you see and be seen – dipped or full beam headlights. So **Answer C** is wrong.

(25)   *Answer D is the right answer.*

9

MOTORWAY RULES

Q. Learner drivers are not allowed on the motorway; so why are there questions on Motorway Rules in the Theory Test for learner drivers?

- As soon as you pass your driving test you will be legally allowed to drive on motorways. You need to know all the rules in advance, so that you are confident and ready to cope with motorway driving when you pass your test.

There are some major roads and dual carriageways that learners can drive on which are very much like motorways. You may drive on some of these fast roads during your driving test, so that your examiner can see how well you cope with hazards at **higher speeds**.

When driving on these fast roads you need some of the same skills that you will need for motorway driving – for example, using **lanes** properly, knowing when it is safe to **overtake**, and **controlling your vehicle** at speed.

- If you are learning to drive with a good driving school, you will have the chance to book a motorway lesson with your instructor after you have passed your test. It makes sense to take up this offer before you drive on a motorway alone for the first time.

FAST TRUX

Q. What are the differences between motorways and other roads?

- On a motorway traffic is **moving at high speed all the time.**

- **All lanes** are in use.

- **No stopping** is allowed on a motorway – traffic only slows or comes to a stop because of accidents or other types of hold-up.

- Some **road users are not allowed on motorways**. These include:

    pedestrians, cyclists and learner drivers

    horses and other animals

    motorcycles under 50cc

    slow-moving vehicles, tractors and farm vehicles

    and invalid carriages.

- You always **leave a motorway on the left**, via a slip road.

- To the left of the inside lane (left-hand lane) on a motorway is an extra lane called the **hard shoulder**. You can only drive on this **in an emergency**.

- Special **signs and signals** are used on motorways.

These include signs above the road on overhead gantries, signs on the central reservation, and amber and red flashing lights.

Checks before your journey

Be extra-careful about doing all your **regular checks** before you set out on a motorway journey; you cannot stop on the motorway to fix small problems, and no one wants to break down in the middle of fast traffic.

Always check:

- the oil and coolant levels

- the screen wash container

- tyres and tyre pressures
- fuel gauge
- that all mirrors and windows are free of dirt and grease
- that the horn works.

Many of these checks are **legally necessary**, as well as **important for your safety**.

How to move on to the motorway

- Join the motorway by **building up your speed on the slip road** to match the speed of traffic in the left lane of the motorway.

- Use **MSM (Mirrors – Signal – Manoeuvre)** and move into the flow of traffic when it is safe to do so.

Changing lanes and overtaking

Driving on a motorway needs all the skills you have learned about **anticipation and forward planning.**

You should

- make good use of all mirrors, and check your blind spots

- signal to move out in plenty of time

- look out for hazards ahead in the lane you want to move to

- not go ahead if it will force another vehicle to brake or swerve

- keep a safe distance from the vehicle in front.

Always ask yourself these three questions before overtaking – especially on motorways:

1. Is it safe?
2. Is it legal?
3. Is it necessary?

Take a break

When you drive on motorways you will sometimes see signs that say 'Tiredness can kill – take a break!'

This is very good advice; motorways are **monotonous** (boring to drive, with long stretches of road that look the same for miles). A major cause of accidents is **drivers falling asleep at the wheel**. Plan your journey so that you have time to get out, stretch your legs and have a drink or snack.

The rules you need to know

- **Keep to the left-hand lane unless you are overtaking** and move back to the left lane as soon as it is safe to do so.

Sometimes you need to stay in the centre lane for a time – for example, when a line of lorries is travelling up a hill in the left lane.

Stay in the centre lane until you have passed the hazard, then signal left and return to the left lane.

- **NEVER**   *reverse*

    park

    walk

    or *drive in the wrong direction* on the motorway.

- Don't **exceed the speed limit.**

This is normally 70mph, but lower speed limits may be signed when the road is busy, or in bad weather.

- Keep to the **correct separation distance** (see pages 42 and 43).

- Don't **overtake on the left.**

If traffic is moving slowly in all three lanes you may find that the lane on the left is moving faster than the one to its right for a short time. Or the left lane may be signed for traffic turning off at the next junction only. But these are exceptions to the rule.

- If luggage falls from your vehicle, **do not get out to pick it up**. Stop at the next emergency phone and tell the police what has happened.

Posts on the edge of the motorway show the way to the nearest emergency phone. You should use these phones rather than your mobile, because the **emergency phone** connects directly to the police and tells them exactly where you are on the motorway.

- **Don't stop on the hard shoulder except in an emergency.**

The hard shoulder is an extremely dangerous place, as many as one in eight road deaths happen there.

RULES FOR USING THE HARD SHOULDER

- Stop as far to the left as possible and, if you can, near an emergency phone.

- Switch on your hazard warning lights.

- Use the left-hand door to get out of the vehicle, and make sure your passengers do too.

- Get everyone away from the road – if possible, behind the barrier or up the bank.

- Leave animals in the vehicle unless they aren't safe there.

- Phone the police with full details of where you are, then go back and wait in a safe place near your vehicle.

Motorway signs

Here are some of the traffic signs you will find on the motorway. These signs are lit up when they are needed to warn you

- that there is an **accident** or a **traffic jam ahead**,

- that a **lane is going to close**

- that a lower speed limit is in force

- that you will have **to cross to the other carriageway** because of roadworks (this is called a '**contraflow**')

- that there is **bad weather** ahead.

SAMPLE QUESTIONS – MOTORWAY RULES

26 **SAMPLE QUESTION**

?

The right way to join a motorway is to

Mark one answer

☐ A drive on the hard shoulder until you see a gap
☐ B come to a stop on the end of the slip road
☐ C speed up to overtake the traffic on your right
☐ D give way to traffic already on the motorway

Working out the answer to Question 26

This question is about three of the rules we have covered in this chapter.

Look back to page 87; the hard shoulder is **only for use in an emergency**, so **Answer A** is wrong.

When joining a motorway you should **build up speed on the slip road** to match that of the traffic in the left lane of the motorway – you **should not come to a stop** before you join the motorway, as you might on non-motorway roads. So **Answer B** is wrong.

Look back to page 86. Speeding up to overtake traffic on your right means the same as **overtaking on the left,** which is not allowed. So **Answer C** is wrong.

Although you should build up your speed to match the traffic already on the motorway, you should not accelerate to race past it – if necessary, you must slow down and **give way** to traffic already on the motorway.

(26) *So Answer D is the right answer.*

(27) SAMPLE QUESTION **Which four of the following are not allowed on motorways?**

Mark four answers

- ☐ **A.** learner drivers
- ☐ **B.** riders of motorcycles above 50cc
- ☐ **C.** tractors
- ☐ **D** bicycles
- ☐ **E** horse riders
- ☐ **F** double-decker buses

Working out the answers to Question 27

If you have learned the information given on page 84 you should have no trouble answering this question.

The only 'catch' is in **Answer B** – 'above 50cc'. You'll remember that motorcycles below 50cc are not allowed on the motorway; but those **above** 50cc *are* allowed.

(27) *Answers A, C, D and E are the four right answers.*

(28) SAMPLE QUESTION

When are you allowed to stop on a motorway?

Mark three answers

- A If you need to check your map
- B Because you are tired and need a break
- C When red lights are showing above every lane
- D When told to stop by the police
- E To answer your mobile phone
- F In an emergency or breakdown

Working out the answers to Question 28

This is a slightly tricky question because the first answer that comes to mind would be 'Never!' – you cannot stop on a motorway.

When you think about it, you know that sometimes you **do** have to stop, for example, if you break down. You must always stop if a person in authority such as a police officer tells you to, or if you see red lights above the road.

(28) *So Answers C, D and F are the three right answers.*

RULES OF THE ROAD

'Rules of the Road' is a good way to describe what is in *The Highway Code*.

The questions that come under this heading in the Theory Test include several on road signs and road markings. There are lots more road sign questions in the section on Road and Traffic Signs.

Several of the topics listed in this section have already come up.

Other questions in this section cover:

- **speed limits**
- **overtaking**
- **parking**
- **lanes and roundabouts**
- **clearways**
- **box junctions**
- **crossroads**
- **pedestrian crossings**
- **towing caravans and trailers.**

Speed limits

Driving too fast for the road, traffic or weather conditions **causes accidents**.

The right speed for the road

Make sure that you **keep below the speed limit shown on the signs for the road you are on.**

(30)

30mph in a built up area

(50)

50mph on a long, twisty country road

(20) ZONE

or as low as 20mph in a residential area with speed humps or traffic calming measures.

The national speed limit for cars on a dual carriageway is 70mph. This is also the maximum speed for motorway driving.

National speed limit

When you leave a built up area you will usually see this sign.

Q. Does this mean I can drive as fast as I like?

- This sign tells you that the national speed limit for this type of road applies here.

- The national speed limit for cars on a normal road (single carriageway outside a built up area) is 60mph.

- So on this road you must drive below 60mph even if it is straight and empty.

The right speed for the conditions

If it is raining or there is snow and ice on the road or if you are driving in a high wind you will have to drive *more slowly than the maximum speed limit*. This will keep you and other road users safe.

- Remember – you have to **double** the time you allow for stopping and braking in wet weather. Allow **even more time** in snow and ice.
- You need to be extra careful when driving in **fog**.

The right speed for your vehicle

Some other vehicles have lower speed limits than cars.

Study this table, and check the section on speed limits in your *Highway Code*.

Type of vehicle	Built-up areas*	Elsewhere		Motorways
		Single carriageways	Dual carriageways	
	MPH	MPH	MPH	MPH
Cars & motorcycles (including car derived vans up to 2 tonnes maximum laden weight)	30	60	70	70
Cars towing caravans or trailers (including car derived vans and motorcycles)	30	50	60	60
Buses & coaches (not exceeding 12 metres in overall length)	30	50	60	70
Goods vehicles (not exceeding 7.5 tonnes maximum laden weight)	30	50	60	70†
Goods vehicles (exceeding 7.5 tonnes maximum laden weight)	30	40	50	60

These are the national speed limits and apply to all roads unless signs show otherwise.
*The 30mph limit applies to all traffic on all roads in England and Wales (only class C and unclassified roads in Scotland) with street lighting unless signs show otherwise.
†60 if articulated or towing a trailer

Parking rules

There are some **general** rules about parking that all drivers should know.

- Whenever you can, you should use off-street car parks, or parking bays. These are marked out with white lines on the road.

- Never park where your vehicle could be a danger to other road users.

PARKING FOR RESIDENTS ONLY

Where not to park

- On the pavement
- At a bus stop
- In front of someone's drive
- Opposite a traffic island
- Near a school entrance
- On a pedestrian crossing (or inside the zig-zag lines either side of the crossing)
- Near a junction
- On a clearway
- On a motorway

Special rules

Look for signs that tell you

- that you cannot park there at certain times of the day
- or that only certain people can park in that place.

Examples:

> *bus lanes*
>
> *cycle lanes*
>
> *residents' parking zones*
>
> *roads edged with red or yellow lines*

Orange or blue badges are given to people with disabilities. Do not park in a space reserved for a disabled driver – **even if that is the only place left to park**. A disabled driver may need to park there. You will break the law if you park in that space.

Parking at night

- If you park at night on a road that has a speed limit higher than 30mph, you must **switch on your parking lights**.

  > You must switch on parking lights **even if you have parked in a lay-by** on this type of road.

- When parking at night, **always park facing in the same direction as the traffic flow**.
- If your vehicle has a **trailer**, you must switch on parking lights, even if the road has a 30mph speed limit.

SAMPLE QUESTIONS – RULES OF THE ROAD

(29) SAMPLE QUESTION

You decide to park your car overnight on a road that has a speed limit of 40mph. You should

Mark one answer

☐ **A** Position your vehicle to face the oncoming traffic

☐ **B** Put your parking lights on before you leave the vehicle

☐ **C** Put dipped headlights on before you leave the vehicle

☐ **D** Park under a street light

Working out the answer to Question 29

When you leave your vehicle in a street overnight, you should park facing **in the same direction as the traffic flow** – not facing the oncoming traffic. So **Answer A** is the wrong answer.

Answer D is partly right. It is always a good idea to choose a well lit parking place, to stop crime. So **Answer D** could be the right answer – unless any of the others is *definitely* right.

To check **Answers B** and **C**, look back to page 95. If you park overnight in road **with a speed limit higher than 30mph** you must **switch on parking lights**. This question is about a road with a **40mph** speed limit.

(29) **So Answer B is the right answer.**

Parking lights are also known as side lights or position lights.

30 SAMPLE QUESTION **You are driving along a street in a town but there are no speed limit signs. How can you tell whether you are in a 30mph area?**

Mark one answer

☐ A By the double yellow lines on the road
☐ B By the pedestrian islands in the middle of the road
☐ C By the hazard warning lines on the road
☐ D By the street lighting

Working out the answer to Question 30

Hazard warning lines do not tell you about speed limits. They tell you to take extra care when overtaking or at junctions. So **Answer C** is wrong.

Double yellow lines (meaning no waiting) or pedestrian islands are often found in busy streets, where you must watch out for pedestrians and other hazards. So **Answers A** and **B** might be right.

However, *The Highway Code* says that the **speed limit where there are street lights is normally 30mph**.

30 *So Answer D is the right answer.*

31 SAMPLE QUESTION **You must not stop on a clearway**

Mark one answer

☐ A At any time
☐ B During the daytime
☐ C Between 4pm and 6pm
☐ D During the night

Working out the answer to Question 31

You can answer this question very easily if you know the road and traffic signs in your *Highway Code*.

The rule for a clearway is simple: no stopping **at any time**.

(31)   *So Answer A is the right answer.*

(32)   **SAMPLE QUESTION**   **You are driving a car towing a trailer on a single carriageway road and you see the sign for National Speed Limit. What is your highest allowed speed?**

Mark one answer

- A   40mph
- B   50mph
- C   60mph
- D   70mph

Working out the answer to Question 32

When you have passed your driving test you will be allowed to tow a small trailer. So you need to know the rules.

Look back to the speed limit table on page 93. You will see that the national speed limit for cars is 70mph on a dual carriageway and 60mph on a single carriageway. Both go down by 10mph when the car is towing a trailer.

(32)   *So the right answer is B – 50mph.*

ROAD AND TRAFFIC SIGNS

Look up the chapter on Road and Traffic Signs in your book of Theory Test questions. You will see that it takes up lots of pages.

- This is because most of the questions have a picture of a road sign or marking.

You will also see that a lot of questions use the same words, but the pictures are different for each question.

- Those words are: *'What does this sign mean?'*

So you can see that you need **to know your** *Highway Code* **very well** to answer the questions in this section.

Q. Will I have to learn The Highway Code off by heart?

- You can try to learn as much of it as possible. There are other ways you can help yourself to get to know the road signs. Look at the next page for some tips on how to get started.

Be aware

As you walk or drive around, **look at the road signs** you see in the street, and the different **markings painted on the road surface**.

If you are on foot:

Look at the signs and signals that all road users must obey, whether they are in a car or walking.

For example, when you use a pedestrian crossing, check what kind of crossing it is (such as a pelican, toucan or zebra crossing).

Check whether you know the following:

- *What are the rules for pedestrians and drivers coming up to the crossing?*
- *What kinds of crossings are controlled by traffic lights?*
- *What is different about a zebra crossing?*

If you are having a driving lesson:

Look well ahead so that you see all the signs that tell you what to do next. Obey them in good time.

Q. Surely in the test the examiner will tell me what to do next?

- When you take your Driving Test the examiner will tell you when to move off, when to make a turn and when to carry out one of the set manoeuvres. But they will expect you to watch out for lane markings on the road, and signs giving directions, and to decide how to react to these yourself.

Q. What should I do when I see lots of signs all in the same place at once?

- If you see several signs all on the same post, it can be confusing. The general rule is to **start at the top** and read down the post.

- The sign at the top tells you about the **first hazard** you have to look out for.

If you are a passenger in a car on a **motorway**, look at the motorway signs, because you need to know them, even though you can't drive on a motorway yet yourself.

Check that you can answer the following:

What colour are the signs at the side of the motorway?
What do the light signals above the road tell you?
What signs tell you that you are coming to an exit?

Know your shapes

Road and traffic signs come in **three main shapes**. Get to know them. You must learn what the signs mean.

Circles

Signs in **circles** tell you **to do** (blue) or **not do** (red) something – they **give orders.**

Triangles

Signs in **triangles** tell you of a **hazard** ahead – they **give warnings.**

> *DID YOU KNOW?*
> There is only one sign which is octagonal – that is, it has eight sides. This is the sign for STOP. The eight-sided shape makes the sign stand out more.
>
> **STOP**

Rectangles

Signs in **rectangles** tell you about **where you are** or **where you are going** – they **give information**.

SAMPLE QUESTIONS – ROAD AND TRAFFIC SIGNS

33 SAMPLE QUESTION

What does this sign mean?

Mark one answer

☐ A Cars and motorcycles only
☐ B No overtaking
☐ C No motor vehicles
☐ D Clearway

Working out the answer to Question 33

This sign shows two vehicles – a car and a motorcycle – in black with a **red circle** round them.

Signs with circles **give orders**; and red tells you **not** to do something (see page 101). So the answer is likely to be one starting with '**No** …'. So **Answer A** is wrong.

The sign for a **clearway** is a red cross on a blue background. So **Answer D** must be wrong.

The sign for **No overtaking** shows a red car next to a black car. So **Answer B** is wrong.

33 *Answer C is the right answer.*

34 SAMPLE QUESTION

Which sign means 'Turn left ahead'?

Mark one answer

A.

B.

C.

D.

Working out the answer to Question 34

All of these signs look similar – they all have white arrows on a blue background.

Make sure you study your *Highway Code* so that you know the difference between similar signs.

There is a clue in the words of the question – 'Turn left ahead'. You must look for the sign which tells you to do something *a little further along the road*.

The arrow in sign **B** goes **up first,** and **then left**.

34 *So Answer B is the right answer.*

The other signs mean:

A – Turn left
C – Keep left
D – Pass either side

(35) SAMPLE QUESTION

This sign means

Mark one answer

- [ ] **A** Tourist attraction
- [ ] **B** Trams crossing ahead
- [ ] **C** Level crossing ahead
- [ ] **D** Beware of trains

Working out the answer to Question 35

You can cross off **Answer B** straight away, because the sign shows a train and not a tram.

Answers C and **D** are both about trains; but the sign for a level crossing is a gate, or a train, in a red triangle. So **Answer C** is wrong.

The shape of this sign tells you it's giving you **information**, instead of a warning or an order. If you've read your *Highway Code*, you should know that tourist attraction signs are usually brown.

(35) *Therefore – A is the right answer.*

12

DOCUMENTS

This is quite a short section in your book of Theory Test questions. It is also different from the other sections, because *it does not deal with driving skills or knowledge of The Highway Code.*

Instead, it covers all the **paperwork** you need to know about when you start learning to drive.

In this section there are questions about:

- driving licences
- insurance
- MOT certificate
- Vehicle Excise Duty (tax disc)
- Vehicle Registration Document (log book)

This section also covers:

- who can supervise a learner driver

and

- changes you must tell the licensing authority about.

Driving licence

If you are learning to drive, you need a provisional licence.

- You must have a **valid** licence to drive legally. 'Valid' means correct, up to date and paid for.

- All licences now have **two parts** – a photocard and a paper document.

- Your signature is on both parts of the licence.

- Take good care of your provisional licence. If you lose it by mistake, you can get another one but you will have to pay a fee, and wait for the new licence to come.

- When you pass your test you can apply for a **full licence**.

Insurance

You must have a valid **insurance certificate** that covers you at least for **third party liability.**

- If you are learning with a good driving school, you are covered by their insurance while you are in the driving school car. When you are in your own or anybody else's car, you must have insurance.

Q. What does 'third party liability' mean?

- Third party insurance cover usually comes as **'Third Party, Fire and Theft'.**

It is a basic insurance policy that will pay for repairs to another person's car and allows you to claim on the other driver's insurance if you are in an accident that was not your fault.

If you have **comprehensive** insurance, the policy will pay for repairs to your vehicle even when the accident was your fault.

MOT certificate

Cars and motorcycles must have their first **MOT test** three years after they are new and first registered. After that, they must have an MOT test every year.

The MOT test checks:

- that your vehicle is **roadworthy** – that is, all the parts work properly and the vehicle is safe to drive

- that it keeps to the legal limits for **exhaust emissions** – that is, the levels of poisons in the gas that comes from the exhaust.

If your vehicle is over three years old you must not drive it without a valid MOT certificate – unless you are on your way to get an MOT and you have booked it in advance.

Vehicle Excise Duty (tax disc)

Your vehicle must have an up to date **tax disc** on the windscreen.

The disc shows that you have paid **Vehicle Excise Duty** up to the date on the disc (you can pay for 6 or 12 months at a time).

Even if you are not driving the car for a while, it must be taxed and have a disc if you keep the vehicle *on the road*.

Q. What does the word 'excise' mean?

- **Vehicle Excise Duty** is the tax that the government charges you to drive your vehicle on the roads. It is also sometimes called **road tax**.

When you get your tax disc, you must show proof that your vehicle is insured, and that it has a valid MOT if required.

> The word excise is easy to confuse with exercise. You will also see it in the term 'Customs and Excise', which means a tax charged on imported goods.

Vehicle Registration Document

The Vehicle Registration Certificate has all the important details about **you and your vehicle,** such as the make and model of the vehicle. It also has your name and address as the **registered keeper** of the vehicle.

It is a record of the vehicle's history and is sometimes called **'the log book'.**

Changes you must tell the licensing authority about

The **Driver and Vehicle Licensing Agency** is known as the **DVLA** for short.

You **must** tell the **DVLA**

- when you buy or sell a car

- or if you change your name or address.

This is because your details go onto the **Vehicle Registration Certificate.**

Supervising a learner driver

Q. Who is allowed to supervise a learner driver?

As a learner driver, you cannot drive on your own. If you are not with your driving instructor, you must be supervised by a person

- who is at least **21 years old**

- and has **a full licence** for the kind of car you drive*

- and has had that licence for **at least three years**.

Note: if a person has a licence to drive an **automatic** car only, they cannot supervise a learner in a **manual** car.

SAMPLE QUESTIONS – DOCUMENTS

36 SAMPLE QUESTION **For how long is an MOT certificate normally valid?**

Mark one answer

- [ ] A 10,000 miles
- [ ] B 30,000 miles
- [ ] C Three years from the date of issue
- [ ] D One year from the date of issue

Working out the answer to Question 36

MOT certificates are not about how many miles the car has travelled. **So Answers A and B** are wrong.

The mention of 'three years' might remind you that the vehicle needs its first MOT three years after it is registered; but **C** is also the wrong answer.

An MOT certificate is valid for one year. When it gets near to the date on the certificate you must book an appointment for your next MOT test.

36 *So Answer D is the right answer.*

37 SAMPLE QUESTION **If someone supervises you while you are learning to drive, how old must they be?**

Mark one answer

- [ ] A Over 18
- [ ] B Over 25
- [ ] C 21 or older
- [ ] D Any age if they have passed their test

Working out the answer to Question 37

It is easy to get this right if you know your *Highway Code.*

Anyone who supervises a learner driver must be at least 21 years old and must have held a full licence for 3 years.

(37) **Therefore – C is the right answer.**

(38) **SAMPLE QUESTION** **What is the minimum insurance cover you MUST have before you drive on the road?**

Mark one answer

- ☐ **A** Third party, fire and theft
- ☐ **B** Fully comprehensive
- ☐ **C** Third party only
- ☐ **D** Excess only

Working out the answer to Question 38

Although third party insurance is usually sold as 'Third Party, Fire and Theft', the law says only that you must have 'a valid insurance certificate covering you for third party liability'.

'Liability' means being responsible for something by law; for example, if you have to pay for the repairs to someone else's car if you have a crash.

(38) **The right answer is C.**

13

ACCIDENTS

The questions in this section are about helping anyone who is hurt in a road accident.

Some people think they might do more harm than good if they try to help. But if you have some knowledge of First Aid you will not panic if you are first on the scene at an accident. You could even save a life.

● Look up Accidents and First Aid in your *Highway Code*.

The Theory Test questions in this section cover:

- what to do when warning lights come on in your vehicle
- what to do if you break down
- safety equipment to carry with you
- when to use hazard warning lights
- what to do – and what not to do – at the scene of an accident.

Basic First Aid

What to do at an accident scene

- Check that you are not putting yourself in danger before you go to help somebody else. You may need to warn other drivers of the accident.

- Check all vehicle engines are switched off.

- Make sure no one is smoking.

- Move people who are not injured to a safe place. If the accident has happened on a motorway, get them away from the hard shoulder, behind the barrier or on to the bank.

- Call the emergency services. You will need to tell them exactly where you are, and how many vehicles are involved in the accident. On motorways, use the emergency phone.

- Do not move injured people – unless there is a risk of fire, or of an explosion.

- Give First Aid to injured people (see below).

- Stay there until the emergency services arrive.

The ABC of First Aid

This tells you what three things to check for when you go to help an injured person:

A **is for Airway**

B **is for Breathing**

C **is for Circulation**

Airway If an injured person is breathing, but unconscious, place them in the recovery position. If they are not breathing, first make sure there is nothing in their mouth that might be blocking the airway.

Breathing If you have checked the airway and they are still not breathing, then give First Aid as follows:

- lift their chin
- carefully tilt their head back to open their airway
- pinch their nose and blow into their mouth until their chest rises.

Repeat this every 4 seconds until the person can breathe alone, or till help arrives.

Circulation 'Circulation' here means 'bleeding'. If a person is bleeding, press firmly on the wound for up to 10 minutes, until the bleeding slows or stops. You can then cover it with a sterile dressing ('sterile' means clean and germ-free). You can raise an injured arm or leg to reduce the bleeding – as long as the limb is not broken.

Other ways to help:

- Do speak in a calm way to the injured person.
- Do try to keep them warm and as comfortable as possible.
- *Do not give them anything to drink.*
- *Do not give them a cigarette.*

Why not learn more about First Aid?
St John Ambulance, St Andrew's Ambulance Assocation
and the British Red Cross all give classes.
You can find their numbers in the phone book.

The AA's advice on safety if you break down

If you are on a non-motorway road:

- Try to get your vehicle off the main road. At least, get it right to the side of the road or on to the verge.
- If the vehicle is in a place where it might be hit by another vehicle, get any passengers out and to a safer place.
- Switch on the hazard warning lights to warn other drivers.
- If you have a red warning triangle, place it at least 45 metres behind your car to warn other traffic (but don't use it on a motorway).
- If you are a member of a motoring organisation such as the AA, call them and tell them where you are and what has happened. Wait with your vehicle until the patrol arrives.

If you are on a motorway:

- If possible, leave the motorway at the next exit. If you can't get that far, drive on to the hard shoulder. Stop far over to the left, and switch on your hazard warning lights.
- Get everyone out of the vehicle, using the nearside doors (but leave pets in the vehicle). Get them to sit on the bank, well away from the traffic.
- Use the nearest orange emergency phone to call the emergency services and tell them where you are and what has happened (for your safety, face the oncoming traffic while you are on the phone).
- Go back to your vehicle and wait on the bank near by until help arrives.
- *Do not:* cross the motorway on foot; or try to do repairs yourself – even changing a wheel. This is too dangerous on a motorway.

SAMPLE QUESTIONS – ACCIDENTS

39 SAMPLE QUESTION **Which three of the following are useful to carry in your car in case you have an accident?**

Mark three answers

- [ ] A Can of fuel
- [ ] B Fire extinguisher
- [ ] C First Aid kit
- [ ] D Red warning triangle
- [ ] E Jump leads
- [ ] F Road atlas

Working out the answers to Question 39

All of these items could be useful. But the question asks for those that are most useful if you are involved in an **accident**.

The First Aid kit and the fire extinguisher are both very important, and the red warning triangle can warn other drivers that a vehicle is causing a hazard. *(But – never place a warning triangle on a motorway.)*

39 *B, C and D are the three right answers.*

40 SAMPLE QUESTION **You are driving on a motorway. When are you allowed to switch on hazard warning lights?**

Mark two answers

- [ ] A When danger ahead causes you to slow down quickly
- [ ] B When towing another vehicle
- [ ] C When driving on the hard shoulder
- [ ] D On the hard shoulder, to warn others that you have broken down
- [ ] E When another vehicle is following you too closely

Working out the answers to Question 40

The Highway Code does not say you should switch on hazard warning lights when towing. But some motorists have got into this habit. **Answer B** is therefore wrong.

As you know by now, the hard shoulder is only for use in an emergency, and you should not drive on it, so **Answer C** is wrong.

If another vehicle is following you too closely you might need to slow down to leave a safer, bigger gap ahead. But you would not use your hazard warning lights in this situation. So **Answer E** is wrong.

(40) *Answers A and D are the two right answers.*

You may switch on hazard warning lights for a short time to let following drivers know there is a hazard.

(41) **SAMPLE QUESTION** **You are at an accident scene and there is someone who is unconscious. Which three things should you check for urgently?**

Mark three answers

- [ ] **A** Broken bones
- [ ] **B** Airway
- [ ] **C** Shock
- [ ] **D** Circulation
- [ ] **E** Breathing

Working out the answers to Question 41

Look back to the 'ABC of First Aid' on page 111, and you have the answer to this question: **B, E and D** – Airway, Breathing and Circulation.

VEHICLE LOADING

This last section, called Vehicle Loading, is the shortest of all. It covers a mixture of the following:

- how to load your vehicle safely
- using a roof rack
- towing caravans and trailers
- child restraints and safety locks.

Q. Why do I need to learn the rules for towing?

- When you have passed your test you can tow a trailer, if the combined weight of the vehicle and trailer is less than 3,500kg. So you need to know the rules about towing.

Towing

When you get your first full driving licence, check it to see how much you are allowed to tow. **Do not tow any trailer that comes to more than that weight.**

The weight of a trailer should be no more than 85% of the weight of the car that is to pull it. But it is best to stay **well below** that top weight, because towing a trailer will **affect the way your vehicle handles.**

> **DID YOU KNOW?**
>
> **A vehicle towing a trailer:**
> - **must not go over a** maximum speed limit of 60mph **(see table, page 93)**
> - **must not use the right** (outside) lane on a motorway.

When you are towing, you need to allow:

- more room when **overtaking**
- more time to **brake and stop**.

When you are turning at a roundabout or junction you will need to think about where you are on the road.

Roof racks

If you put a roof rack on your car, it will make a difference to **the way your vehicle handles**.

- The roof rack makes your vehicle taller, so more vulnerable to strong winds.
- You will increase your fuel consumption (use more fuel).
- You need to change the way you drive to allow for the extra weight.

Any load that is carried on a roof rack **must be tied down securely**.

> When towing a heavy load, you might need to blow your tyres up to more than the normal pressures. Check your vehicle's handbook for advice. Remember to change back to the normal pressures when you finish your journey.

To find out more, look up the parts of your *Highway Code* that deal with **Loads** and **Towing** (don't confuse 'Loads' with 'Loading and Unloading', which is about vehicles making deliveries).

Loading a trailer

If the weight of the load is arranged properly, this should cut down the risk of **losing control, swerving and snaking** (see below).

- Try to **spread the weight evenly** when you load your trailer. Do not put more weight towards the front, or the back, or to one side.

- Remember – it is **against the law** to have a load that is **sticking out in a dangerous way**.

- Don't forget that if you park a vehicle with a trailer overnight, it must have **lights**.

Snaking

'Snaking' means moving from side to side. A caravan will snake if it is not properly attached or loaded, or if the car pulling it is going too fast.

> **DID YOU KNOW?**
> If you are going to buy a trailer, make sure it fits your car's tow bar. Tow bars must keep to EU regulations, and must have electric sockets to connect to the lights on the trailer.

If you are towing a caravan or trailer and it starts to snake:

- slow down – stop pressing the accelerator (do not brake suddenly)
- get back in control of the steering
- then brake gently.

The driver's responsibility for the passengers

There are also questions in this section about the safety of passengers.

As the driver, you are responsible for **making sure your vehicle is not overloaded** – and this applies to **people and animals** as well as to luggage.

All passengers:

- must wear a **seat belt** (unless they have a medical certificate saying they should not wear one)
- all children under 14 must wear a seat belt or be strapped into a **child seat** or other 'restraint' suitable for their age. (See the section on Child Restraints in your *Highway Code*.)

Children must not sit in the **space behind the back seat** of a hatchback car, and no passengers should **sit in a caravan** while it is being towed.

Pets should be kept under careful control. You might keep them safe with a special harness, or behind a screen in a hatchback to stop them being thrown forward in an accident.

SAMPLE QUESTIONS – VEHICLE LOADING

42 **SAMPLE QUESTION** **What should you do if the trailer you are towing starts to snake or swerve?**

Mark one answer

- [ ] A Reduce speed by easing off the accelerator
- [ ] B Let go of the steering wheel so that the vehicle can correct itself
- [ ] C Speed up to drive out of the swerving
- [ ] D Brake hard and keep the brake pedal down

Working out the answer to Question 42

Look back to the advice on snaking on pages 119-20. You should reduce speed – stop pressing the accelerator, as in **Answer A**. To let go of the steering wheel (**Answer B**) would of course be extremely dangerous. Speeding up or braking hard (**C and D**) will both make the problem worse.

42 *So Answer A is the right answer.*

43 **SAMPLE QUESTION** **Your passengers ask if they can ride in a caravan while you are towing it. Are they allowed to do this?**

Mark one answer

- [ ] A Yes, if they are all over 14
- [ ] B Yes, if all the seats in the car are full
- [ ] C No, not at any time
- [ ] D Yes, as long as you are not on a motorway.

Working out the answer to Question 43

You are responsible for seeing that all your passengers are safe. You must not let them ride in a towed caravan at any time.

 43 | ***So Answer C is the right answer.***

You should also check that all your passengers are wearing their seat belts, and that children are belted into child seats or child restraints.

44 **SAMPLE QUESTION** **You should not overload your vehicle as the excess weight will affect the**

Mark two answers

- [ ] **A** battery
- [ ] **B** gearbox
- [ ] **C** handling
- [ ] **D** journey time
- [ ] **E** steering

Working out the answers to Question 44

You need to use some different driving skills when your vehicle is heavily loaded, when you have a roof rack fitted, or when you are towing a trailer. The vehicle may not respond as well as usual, and you might find that the steering feels different.

 44 | ***So Answers C and E – vehicle handling and steering – are the two right answers.***

KEY WORDS

Accelerate
To make the vehicle move faster by pressing the right-hand pedal.

Adverse weather
Bad weather that makes driving difficult or dangerous.

Alert
Quick to notice possible hazards.

Anticipation
Looking out for hazards and taking action before a problem starts.

Anti-lock brakes
Brakes that stop the wheels locking so that you are less likely to skid on a slippery road.

Aquaplane
To slide out of control on a wet road surface.

Articulated vehicle
A long vehicle that is divided into two or more sections joined by cables.

Attitude
The way you think or feel, which affects the way you drive. Especially, whether you are patient and polite, or impatient and aggressive.

Automatic car
A vehicle with gears that change by themselves as you speed up or slow down.

Awareness
Taking notice of the road and traffic conditions around you at all times.

Blind spot
The section of road behind you which you cannot see in your mirrors. You 'cover' your blind spot by looking over your shoulder before moving off or overtaking.

Brake fade
Loss of power to the brakes when you have been using them for a long time without taking your foot off the brake pedal. For example, when driving down a steep hill. The brakes will overheat and not work properly.

Braking distance
The distance you must allow to slow the vehicle in order to come to a stop.

Brow of a hill
The highest point of a hill.

Carriageway
One side of a road or motorway. A 'dual carriageway' has two lanes on each side of a central reservation.

Catalytic converter
A piece of equipment fitted in the exhaust system that changes harmful gases into less harmful ones.

Chicane
A sharp double bend that has been put into a road to make traffic slow down.

Child restraint
A child seat or special seat belt for children. It keeps them safe and stops them moving around in the car.

Clearway
A road where no stopping is allowed at any time. The sign for a clearway is a red cross in a red circle on a blue background.

Coasting
Letting the vehicle run down hill without using any of the gears. That is, with your foot on the clutch pedal or the car in neutral.

Commentary driving
Talking to yourself about what you see on the road ahead and what action you are going to take.

Comprehensive insurance
A motor insurance policy that pays for repairs even if you cause an accident.

Concentration
Keeping all your attention on your driving.

Conditions
How good or bad the road surface is, how much traffic is on the road, and what the weather is like.

Congestion
Heavy traffic that makes it difficult to get to where you want to go.

Consideration
Thinking about other road users and not just yourself. For example, letting another driver go first at a junction, or stopping at a zebra crossing to let pedestrians cross over.

Contraflow
When traffic on a motorway follows signs to move to the opposite carriageway for a short distance because of roadworks. (During a contraflow, there is traffic driving in both directions on the same side of the motorway.)

Coolant
Liquid in the radiator that removes heat from the engine.

Defensive driving
Driving safely without taking risks, looking out for hazards and thinking for others.

Disqualified
Stopped from doing something (eg driving) by law, because you have broken the law.

Distraction
Anything that stops you concentrating on your driving, such as chatting to passengers or on your mobile phone.

Document
An official paper or card, such as your driving licence.

Dual carriageway
One side of a road or motorway, with two lanes on each side of a central reservation.

Engine braking
Using the low gears to keep your speed down. For example, when you are driving down a steep hill and you want to stop the vehicle

running away. Using the gears instead of braking will help to prevent brake fade.

Environment
The world around us and the air we breathe.

Exhaust emissions
Gases that come out of the exhaust pipe to form part of the outside air.

Field of vision
How far you can see in front and around you when you are driving.

Ford
A place in a stream or river which is shallow enough to drive across with care.

Frustration
Feeling annoyed because you cannot drive as fast as you want to because of other drivers or heavy traffic.

Fuel consumption
The amount of fuel (petrol or diesel) that your vehicle uses. Different vehicles have different rates of consumption. Increased fuel consumption means using more fuel. Decreased fuel consumption means using less fuel.

Fuel gauge
A display or dial on the instrument panel that tells you how much fuel (petrol or diesel) you have left.

Gantry
An overhead platform like a high narrow bridge that displays electric signs on a motorway.

Handling
How well your vehicle moves when you steer or brake.

Harass
To drive in a way that makes other road users afraid.

Hard shoulder
The single lane to the left of the inside lane on a motorway, which is for emergency use only.

You should not drive on the hard shoulder except in an emergency, or when there are signs telling you to use the hard shoulder because of roadworks.

Harsh braking (or harsh acceleration)
Using the brake or accelerator too hard so as to cause wear on the engine.

Hazard warning lights
Flashing amber lights which you should use only when you have broken down. On a motorway you can use them to warn other drivers behind of a hazard ahead.

High-sided vehicle
A van or truck with tall sides, or a tall trailer such as a caravan or horse-box, that is at risk of being blown off-course in strong winds.

Impatient
Not wanting to wait for pedestrians and other road users.

Inflate
To blow up – to put air in your tyres until they are at the right pressures.

Intimidate
To make someone feel afraid.

Involved
Being part of something. For example, being one of the drivers in an accident.

Jump leads
A pair of thick electric cables with clips at either end. You use it to charge a flat battery by connecting it to the live battery in another vehicle.

Junction
A place where two or more roads join.

Liability
Being legally responsible.

MOT
The test that proves your car is safe to drive. Your MOT certificate is one of the important documents for your vehicle.

Manoeuvre
Using the controls to make your car move in a particular direction. For example turning, reversing or parking.

Manual
By hand. So in a car that is a 'manual' or has manual gears, you have to change the gears yourself (see Automatic, above).

Maximum
The largest possible; 'maximum speed' is the highest speed allowed.

Minimum
The smallest possible.

Mobility
The ability to move around easily.

Monotonous
Boring. For example, a long stretch of motorway with no variety and nothing interesting to see.

Motorway
A fast road that has two or more lanes on each side and a hard shoulder. Drivers must join or leave it on the left, via a motorway junction. Many kinds of slower vehicles – such as bicycles – are not allowed on motorways.

Multiple-choice questions
Questions with several possible answers where you have to try to choose the right one.

Observation
The ability to notice important information, such as hazards developing ahead.

Obstruct
To get in the way of another road user.

Octagonal
Having eight sides.

Pedestrian
A person walking.

Pegasus crossing
An unusual kind of crossing. It has a button high up for horse riders to push (Pegasus was a flying horse in Greek legend).

Pelican crossing
A crossing with traffic lights that pedestrians can use by pushing a button. Cars must give way to pedestrians on the crossing while the amber light is flashing. You must give pedestrians enough time to get to the other side of the road.

Perception
Seeing or noticing (as in Hazard Perception).

Peripheral vision
The area around the edges of your field of vision.

Positive attitude
Being sensible and obeying the law when you drive.

Practical Driving Test
The part of the test, taken in a vehicle, which is about driving skills.

Priority
The vehicle or other road user that is allowed by law to go first is the one that has priority.

Provisional licence
A first driving licence. All learner drivers must get one before they start having lessons.

Puffin crossing
A type of pedestrian crossing that does not have a flashing amber light phase.

Reaction time
The amount of time it takes you to see a hazard and decide what to do about it.

Red route
You see these in London and some other cities. Double red lines at the edge of the road tell you that you must not stop or park there at any time. Single red lines have notices with times when you must not stop or park. Some red routes have marked bays for either parking or loading at certain times.

Red warning triangle
An item of safety equipment to carry in your car in case you break down. You can place the triangle 45m behind your car on the same side of the road. It warns traffic that your vehicle is causing an obstruction. (Do not use these on motorways.)

Residential areas
Areas of housing where people live. The speed limit is 30mph or sometimes 20mph.

Rumble strips
Raised strips across the road near a roundabout or junction that change the sound the tyres make on the road surface, warning drivers to slow down. They are also used on motorways to separate the main carriageway from the hard shoulder.

Safety margin
The amount of space you need to leave between your vehicle and the one in front so that you are not in danger of crashing into it if the driver slows down suddenly or stops. Safety margins have to be longer in wet or icy conditions.

Separation distance
The amount of space you need to leave between your vehicle and the one in front so that you are not in danger of crashing into it if the driver slows down suddenly or stops. The separation distance must be longer in wet or icy conditions.

Single carriageway
Generally, a road with one lane in each direction.

Snaking
Moving from side to side. This sometimes happens with caravans or trailers when you drive too fast, or they are not properly loaded.

Staggered junction
Where you drive across another road. Instead of going straight across, you have to go slightly to the right or left.

Sterile
Clean and free from bacteria.

Stopping distance
The time it takes for you to stop your vehicle – made up of 'thinking distance' and 'braking distance'.

Supervisor
Someone who sits in the passenger seat with a learner driver. They must be over 21 and have held a full driving licence for at least three years.

Tailgating
Driving too closely behind another vehicle – either to harass the driver in front or to make yourself feel safer in thick fog.

Tax disc
The disc you show on your windscreen to prove that you have taxed your car (see Vehicle Excise Duty, below).

Thinking distance
The time it takes you to notice something and take the right action. You need to add thinking distance to your braking distance to make up your total stopping distance.

Third party insurance
A minimal insurance policy that will pay for damage to someone else's property if you have an accident.

Toucan crossing
A type of pedestrian crossing that does not have a flashing amber light phase. Cyclists are allowed to ride across.

Tow
To pull something behind your vehicle. It could be a caravan or trailer.

Traffic calming measures
Speed humps, chicanes and other devices placed in roads to slow traffic down.

Tread depth
The depth of the grooves in a car's tyres that help them grip the road surface. The grooves must all be at least 1.6mm deep.

Turbulence
Strong movement of air. For example, when a large vehicle passes a much smaller one.

Two-second rule
In traffic that's moving at normal speed, allow at least a two-second gap between you and the vehicle in front.

Tyre pressures
The amount of air which must be pumped into a tyre in order for it to be correctly blown up.

Vehicle Excise Duty
The tax you pay for your vehicle so that you may drive it on public roads.

Vehicle Registration Certificate
A record of details about a vehicle and its owner.

Vulnerable
At risk of harm or injury.

Waiting restrictions
Times when you may not park or load your vehicle in a particular area.

Wheel spin
When the vehicle's wheels spin round out of control with no grip on the road surface.

Zebra crossing
A pedestrian crossing without traffic lights. It has an orange light, and is marked by black and white stripes on the road. Drivers must stop for pedestrians to cross.

INDEX